MW01196437

# THE
# MYSTErY
## Of ISrQEL

Other books by this author:
*Secrets of Daniel*
*Secrets of Revelation*

To order, **call 1-800-765-6955.**

Visit us at www.reviewandherald.com for information on other Review and Herald® products.

# THE
# MYSTERY
# OF ISRAEL

## JACQUES B. DOUKHAN

REVIEW AND HERALD® PUBLISHING ASSOCIATION
HAGERSTOWN, MD 21740

The author assumes full responsibility for the accuracy of all facts and quotations as cited in this book.

This book was
Edited by Gerald Wheeler
Copyedited by Delma Miller and James Cavil
Cover designed by Willie Duke/Leumas Design
Cover photos by Getty Images
Electronic makeup by Shirley M. Bolivar
Typeset: 11/15 Bembo

PRINTED IN U.S.A.

08  07  06          5  4  3  2

**R&H Cataloging Service**
Doukhan, Jacques B. 1940-    .
    The mystery of Israel

1. Jews—Election, Doctrine of.  I. Title.

296.3

ISBN 10: 0-8280-1772-7
ISBN 13: 978-0-8280-1772-5

# contents

"And the people of the prince . . . shall destroy the city and
the sanctuary" (verse 26)
Excursus: a rabbinic curse about Daniel

# Introduction

Prussian King Frederick II one day asked his personal physician, "Could you give me at least one single evidence of the existence of God?" The man answered, "Your Majesty, the Jews." This classic story speaks loudly about the "mystery of Israel."

All great ancient civilizations such as Egypt, Rome, and Greece have disappeared. Only the Jews have survived as a cultural identity in spite of pogroms, persecutions, and all other attempts to exterminate them, including the Holocaust. From biblical times with Moses, Isaiah, Jesus, and Paul to modern times with Marx, Freud, and Einstein, Jews have always been prominent in history. And they are still in the news, more than ever because of the state of Israel. The Jews are less than 0.5 percent of the world's population, yet they capture a huge place in humanity's attention. "Are the non-Jews victims of a hallucination?" wonders Christian theologian Fadiey Lovsky.[1] A real mystery indeed that puzzles and disturbs many Christians. The word "mystery" in regard to Israel troubles many. The concept may suggest a hidden and bizarre meaning beyond our understanding. It may also imply suspicion and fears toward the unknown, thus inspiring anti-Semitic myths and theories. Significantly, many have used the expression "mystery of Israel" in the context of a theology of rejection and curse on Israel. For Paul, however, who first applied the expression to Israel, it meant something positive. Romans 11:25 associates it with the need to dissipate ignorance: "I do not desire, brethren, that you should be ignorant of this mystery." The word "mystery," then, points to a special revelation. Indeed, in most New Testament instances in which the word "mystery" appears, it is "coupled with words of manifesting and divulging."[2] Searching out the "mystery of Israel" means more than a mere intellectual exercise of trying to decode the strange historical phenomenon of Israel. It pertains to God's revelation and therefore involves the task of theology. And since this expression belongs to a passage that is dealing with a prophecy and mission that concern Israel, writing a theology of Israel implies, by necessity, learning about prophecy and mission.

Scholars have written much about Israel but have done very little work on the theology of Israel as such. Too often what they have produced is little more than an opportunity to indulge in sensationalism or a dangerously superficial sketch full of historical and theological confusion and ethical problems. The few Seventh-day Adventist theologies of Israel[3] proposed so far have been lacking in three areas:

1. These theologies of Israel have often adopted the traditional theory of rejection and supersessionism without providing serious exegesis of the biblical sources used to support it.

2. The strong apologetic concern of some Seventh-day Adventist theologians and evangelists against the dispensationalist theory has led them to overemphasize the idea of God's rejection of Israel and even a curse upon the Jews. At times implicitly or explicitly anti-Semitic, this position promotes very

little, if any, awareness of or sensitivity toward the human reality of the Jewish people and fails to take into account the lessons of history, such as the Holocaust.

3. The teaching of rejection and supersessionism is somewhat inconsistent with the specific perspective of Seventh-day Adventist ecclesiology. It is not compatible with the Adventist recognition and condemnation of the failure and theological apostasy of the historical church (its oppression toward dissenters, and its rejection of God's law and the Sabbath) and ultimately with the Seventh-day Adventist prophetic identity and eschatological role toward the church and Israel as the "repairer of the breach."[4]

Indeed, these deficiencies are serious enough to call for further study and reflection on the matter. The purpose of the present work is to engage in a direction that is more biblically, exegetically, and theologically correct, and that provides a more sensitive, Adventist view of Israel.

I will proceed in four steps. First, I will discuss successively the two traditional theologies of Israel, the rejection-supersessionism theory and the dispensationalist theory, addressing the main biblical texts traditionally used to support the respective theories. My approach will be essentially exegetical, to ensure that the biblical data[5] control both our theology of Israel and our *prophetic* interpretations. Then, on the basis of this discussion, I will suggest a third theory, which will take into consideration the historical accident of the Christian apostasy and related Jewish-Christian separation. I will examine the issue in regard to the specific prophetic and eschatological identity and *mission* of the Seventh-day Adventist Church toward the Christian church at large and Israel in particular. Only at the end, in light of all the data, shall we be able to unlock the mystery of Israel.

And from that perspective, we shall learn *our* lessons and evaluate *our* spiritual journey as Israel.

---

[1] *La déchirure de l'absence: Essai sur les rapports entre l'Église du Christ et le peuple d'Israël* (Paris: Calmann-Lévy, 1971), p. 8. Author's translation.

[2] *The Interpreter's Dictionary of the Bible,* vol. 3, p 480.

[3] This essay will not identify these works because (1) I do not wish to place this reflection and this research on the level of a personal dispute, and (2) because I do not want to misrepresent their positions. After all, everyone should be able to recognize themselves in this description and then respond accordingly.

[4] Isa. 58:12; see Ellen G. White, *Testimonies for the Church* (Mountain View, Calif.: Pacific Press Pub. Assn., 1948), vol. 1, pp. 76, 77.

[5] Considering the importance of Ellen White's impact on Seventh-day Adventist theology, I have also consulted her along the way when I judged it necessary to support or orient our interpretation. My references to Ellen White's writings will, however, remain only incidental in this study, as I have devoted the appendix to the topic of Ellen White and the Jews.

*Section I*

# The Rejection-Supersessionist Theory

The oldest thesis, the rejection-supersessionist theory is ultimately the most persistent one. It appears for the first time in the writings of the Church Fathers, and Christian theologians of many viewpoints have aggressively elaborated it. From Justin Martyr, Augustine, and Thomas Aquinas to Martin Luther and Rudolf Bultmann, its proponents have based this traditional theory on a simple rationale: *Israel has failed*.[1] It teaches that the disobedience of the people of Israel in the Old Testament and, above all, in the New Testament with the rejection and crucifixion of the Messiah, has led God to reject Israel and make a "new covenant" with a new people. The Israel of the Old Testament stands replaced by the Christian church, which has inherited all the privileges and divine blessings given to Abraham and the Hebrew prophets, leaving to the Jews only the curses and the judgments.

Today, reflecting upon Auschwitz, more and more people have come to recognize the damage done by the rejection theory. We now know this thesis has consciously and dangerously nurtured the "teaching of contempt" and inspired the anti-

Semitic hatred that led to the Nazi Holocaust.[2] In a monstrous manner some have employed this theology as a religious justification for the suffering of the Jews. Even worse, some have seen in it a religious justification for the suffering of the Jews (by the way, always perpetrated by the Christians), and even for the horror of the concentration camps and the gas chambers.

The idea of replacement or supersession,[3] a concept implied in the rejection theory, has also been used to excuse theological distortions (i.e., theological supersessionism) and ecclesiastical and political abuses (i.e., ecclesiastical supersessionism) directed toward Jews.

Theological supersessionism, found especially in European Protestantism, favors the idea that the New Testament has replaced the Old. Further, grace has replaced law, and the spiritual God of salvation in the New Testament has replaced the carnal God of Creation in the Old. Sunday, the celebration of spiritual deliverance from the evil of nature and the body, has replaced the seventh-day Sabbath, the biblical institution celebrating Creation. While these views find their origins in the second-century heresy of Marcion, they continue to persist in traditional Christian thought.

Ecclesiastical supersessionism, found especially in Catholicism, first inspired the Crusaders, who believed that Jerusalem was now the Christians' heritage, as well as the medieval destruction of synagogues and the building of Christian churches on their sites. Thus, the psychological mechanism of ecclesiastical supersessionism has the potential for murder. Further, to claim that we as Christians have replaced the Jews is to suggest that Jews have no right to exist from a spiritual perspective: they are spiritually superfluous. Some Christians, such as Franklin H.

Littell, have been led to decry this concept as "spiritual genocide."[4] According to historians of anti-Semitism, ecclesiastical
supersessionism, combined with general Christian indifference,
was the greatest motivation behind the destruction of the Jews
during the Holocaust.

The development in the third century of Manichaenism, a
form of religious dualism that asserted that everything material
and sensual is evil and must be overcome, proposed yet another
form of supersessionism. The theory proposed that the Christian
church was the true "spiritual Israel," representing God and
good, in opposition to the false "carnal Israel," which represented Satan and evil. This view has not only encouraged dangerous anti-Semitic stereotypes about the "carnal and deceitful
Jew," but also promoted a dualistic, and therefore biblically suspect, contrast between what is carnal and transitory and what is
spiritual and enduring.

Even the typological approach, which represents the most
positive variation of supersessionist theory, may sometimes lead
to confusion insofar as it ignores or weakens the historical and
theological reality of Israel. For instance, if Israel is only a "type"
of the Christian church—an example to follow or not to follow—Israel is reduced to the empty status of a shadow, the reality of which blossoms only within the church. Another
weakness of the typological approach is the identification of
Israel with Jesus. Although the Bible attests to the corporate
view that associates Israel with its Redeemer (e.g., Isa. 53; Dan.
7; 9), the distinction between the two is clear and should always
be present in order to safeguard a healthy tension. Otherwise,
the creature is erased at the expense of the Creator, or, as illustrated in the writings of Teilhard de Chardin, a subtle panthe-

ism is introduced, in which the distance between God and the creature has disappeared, with the result that Israel, the church, has become the *omega,* Jesus, God Himself.

Advocates of the rejection-supersessionist theory have used a number of key texts and/or themes from the Old and New Testament to support it. We shall now discuss them.

## 1. THE FAILURE OF OLD TESTAMENT ISRAEL

Two primary Old Testament texts have traditionally served as claims that God has rejected Israel of the Old Testament. The first is the story of the Israelites who asked for a king.[5] "They have rejected Me" (1 Sam. 8:7), God states. From this divine declaration rejectionist and supersessionist proponents have concluded that God has abandoned Israel. But the rest of the story—the anointing of a king by a prophet sent by God, the promise of the Messiah, the Anointed One, descendant of the Israelite King David, and the continuous history of God with His people—clearly demonstrates that God did not abandon His people at that time.

Another favorite text of the rejection theorists is the prophecy of Hosea, which identifies Israel with the sacred prostitute of the Canaanite cult whose son received the new name Lo-Ammi ("not my people" [Hosea 1:9]). They have also inferred from the story that Israel, now a prostitute, was no longer God's wife and had been rejected by Him. The prophet Hosea, however, still remained the prostitute Gomer's husband and returned to her in spite of her unfaithfulness—a sign of God's great faithfulness to His unfaithful people. Ironically, texts that God intended to demonstrate His free love and mercy have been used to show God's rejection. Such interpreters put the accent on the sinful state of the prostitute when it belonged, in fact, on God, who remains the loving husband despite what the wife has done. In the history of Israel God continues to pursue His people with His love. Prophets arose (e.g., Jeremiah, Ezekiel, Haggai), and God continued to protect the people[6] (Esther, Daniel), ultimately restoring them to Jerusalem (Ezra, Nehemiah) in spite of the people's unfaithfulness and God's warnings and judgments.

Now, the fact that the people still remain God's chosen people in spite of their unfaithfulness does not mean that all the people will succeed and that all will be saved no matter what. We should distinguish between the notion of election and salvation. The unfaithful may not be saved, but they are still a part of the chosen people that witnesses to God's plan of salvation. Further, the notion of the "remnant," developed especially by the eighth-century prophets, does not necessarily imply "rejection" of the rest of the people. The remnant is still a part of the chosen people and is, in fact, a sign that Israel remains the chosen people. The remnant are the faithful who within the chosen people will survive the test of God's judgment and who will ultimately enjoy the eschatological reward of salvation. We should not, however, identify the "remnant" with the "chosen people." Not all of the Israelites were a part of the remnant (1 Kings 19:18), and not all the remnant belonged to the chosen people of Israel (Isa. 46:3; 45:20; 66:19).

## 2. THE PARABLE OF THE VINEYARD

Of all the stories Jesus told, the parable of the vineyard (Matt. 21:33-46) is one of the most often quoted. Many have interpreted the rejection of the vinedressers, who did not take care of the vine and even killed the son of the landowner, and the reaction of the owner, who leases "His vineyard to other vinedressers" (Matt. 21:41), as the dismissal and the replacement of the people of Israel. However, we need to note that when Jesus explains, "The kingdom of God will be taken from you and given to a nation bearing the fruits of it" (verse 43), He is *addressing specifically* the leaders who were present, the chief priests and Pharisees who clearly understood that He had them in mind. "When the chief priests and Pharisees heard His parables, they perceived that He was speaking of them" (verse 45). To use this parable to defend the idea that God has cast off the Jewish *people* and replaced them with the Christian church does not do justice to Jesus' own explanation of the parable. Indeed, when He refers to "the kingdom of God" that will be taken from them, He does not have in mind the election of Israel. Instead, Jesus is speaking of the issue of salvation, as the expression "kingdom of God" suggests (see Matt. 19:23, 24). His point is not that God has rejected Israel and substituted another people. As John Bright in his book *The Kingdom of God* comments, the expression "kingdom of God" on the lips of Jesus involved "the whole notion of the rule of God over his people, and particularly the vindication of that rule and people in glory at the end of history. That was the Kingdom which the Jews awaited." [7] The message of the kingdom of God is that of salvation. Jesus' point to the chief priests and the Pharisees concerns not their election but rather their salvation. When Jesus speaks to them of the "kingdom of God" being removed from them and given to others, He means that He has had to take the salvation they are spurning and offer it to others.

Who are these others to whom salvation has been given? The

Greek word *ethnos,* here translated as "nations," actually renders the Hebrew word *goy,* which designates Gentiles (see Matt. 4:15; 6:32; Acts 26:17; Rom. 3:29; 11:11; 15:10)[8] or the Gentile Christians (Rom. 11:13; 15:27; 16:4; Gal. 2:12, 14; Eph. 3:1). It is also significant that the First Letter of Peter applies *ethnos* to the prophecy of Hosea (Hosea 2:1-23) and uses it with precisely the same meaning to the Gentiles: "Who once were not a people but are now the people of God, who had not obtained mercy but now have obtained mercy" (1 Peter 2:10). As far as the parable is concerned, "it may well be," Jesus says, "that you will not be saved—you will not enter the kingdom of God, while the Gentile, the *goy [ethnos],* will be saved." In the preceding parable of the two sons (Matt. 21:28-31) Jesus specifically refers to the chief priests: "Assuredly, I say to you that tax collectors and harlots enter the kingdom of God before you" (verse 31). The rhetorical language in Matthew 21:43 ("The kingdom of God will be taken away from you and given to a people who will produce its fruit" [NIV]) does not suggest that all the Jews as such are lost (or have been divinely rejected as chosen people) and replaced by another Gentile "nation." Nor do these texts suggest that only tax collectors and harlots will be saved or elected. In this parable Jesus aims His statement at the chief priests, the "tenants" or "vinedressers," who are the corrupt Temple leadership. He does not imply either the rejection or the loss of the rest of the Jewish people. In fact, it could not be the case, since verse 46 describes the Jewish people as "multitudes" whom the leaders "feared . . . because they took Him for a prophet."[9] We must, therefore, make a clear distinction between these leaders (which, by the way, did not include *all* the religious leaders, as some were sympathetic to the gospel, and many of them later accepted Jesus)[10] and the Jewish people.[11] Flavius Josephus,[12]

Talmudic,[13] and Qumran[14] sources confirm this distinction and emphasize that the general population abhorred the Jewish leaders at that time, especially the priests, and did not consider them their legal or even spiritual representatives.[15]

Thus the argument of "corporate personality," which is sometimes used to support the idea of the responsibility of the Jewish people for the sins of their leaders, stumbles on important considerations.

*The historical context of the New Testament.* The Jewish people were then under occupation by a foreign power (the Romans), and their leaders were not accepted ones (see above). The Romans had appointed some of them or allowed them to gain power.

*The theological context of the new covenant.* The perspective of the new covenant in Jesus Christ no longer functions within corporate ethnic categories. It is also ironic that those who emphasize the idea of corporate ethnic punishment against Israel insist, on the other hand, on the contrast between the universal-individual nature of the new covenant and the corporate nature of the old covenant. In other words, when arguing for Israel's punishment, they apply the principle of corporate personality; but when they discuss the salvation of the Gentiles, they reject that principle and embrace the universal-individual principle. Such contradiction and inconsistency speaks for itself.

*The biblical view of God.* The Bible testifies to a God who does not punish the righteous with the wicked (Gen. 18:23; Matt. 13:29).

*The ethical embarrassment.* The idea of collective guilt and punishment would have terrible implications in our reading of history. Not only would it imply the justification of the Holocaust (contemporary European Jews being punished for the crime of the Crucifixion); it would also call for the guilt and responsibility of all Europeans (especially Germans and Austrians) for the Nazi iniquity. Or more recently, it would demand the responsibility of all Adventist Rwandans (if not all Adventists) for the Rwandan holocaust, since some Adventist leaders participated in the massacres.

*The sociological/anthropological consideration.* Indeed, the principle of corporate personality does operate in a tribal society, as attested in the ancient Near East[16] and in the Bible (Joshua 7; 2 Sam. 24:1-7). It would be, however, highly inappropriate to elevate the axiom to an absolute and universal principle that "should" apply to any society at any time. Already in New Testament times Israelite culture was no longer the tribal society it was as ancient Israel. The great majority of Jewish people now lived in the Diaspora (Dispersion), many of the Palestinian Jews had lost track of their tribal identity, and more important, Israelite society was no longer united under the "theocratic" rule of a king. In fact, the example of Ananias and Sapphira shows clearly that the principle of corporate personality no longer remained in operation. While in ancient Israel the iniquity of the individual—Achan, for example—could affect the entire nation, the sin of Ananias and Sapphira and the divine judgment that resulted did not have an impact on the nation of Israel as a whole, but affected only themselves and the specific group (the church) they belonged to.

Jesus' association of the crimes of the Pharisees with the crimes of Cain and King Joash in Matthew 23:35 do not express a corporate personality. Cain was not the ancestor of the scribes and the Pharisees, nor of King Joash. Jesus links these individuals together only on the basis of the similarity of their iniquity by the association of ideas, not on the principle of corporate personality. Otherwise, if the concept of corporate personality or "the notion of communal solidarity"[17] was implicit in Jesus' words, it would suggest that the Pharisees and the Jewish people they represent could be accountable for the crime of Cain, and hence for any crime in human history at any time and any place. In fact, the idea of collective punishment that would affect the innocent along with the culprit violates divine principles (see Ex. 23:7). To interpret this passage in support of collective punishment is essentially a human reaction of revenge that has nothing to do with the principle of "corporate personality" and pertains rather to pagan and barbaric culture as exemplified by the Persian king Darius (Dan. 6:24).

Even if God had directed His judgment toward the Jewish people of that time as a whole, not only because of the sins of their leaders but also because of their own sins, this does not necessarily mean that corporate rejection took place. Never throughout the history of Israel had judgment implied collective exclusion. On the contrary, it implied God's faithful attention and loving interest in His people when He called them to repentance (e.g., Hosea 5; 6; Isa. 1:18). Likewise, at the end of time God's people identified as Laodicea (meaning "judgment of the people") are judged because of their self-righteousness and tepidnes. This does not mean that God will spurn them corporately. On the contrary, He gives this judgment to them in order to enable them to understand that "as many as I [God] love, I rebuke and chasten" (Rev. 3:19), with the incentive to have zeal and repent (see verse 19).

The narrative of the vineyard is a parable, and as such it is stylistically designed to allow for a variety of interpretations. The least that we can infer from our discussion is a need to exercise caution. It would not be wise to build a dogmatic theology on this story.

## 3. THE CRIME OF DEICIDE

It is primarily the accusation of deicide that has served as the main justification for the rejection theory. According to this view, the majority of the Jews were responsible for the crucifixion and rejection of Jesus as the Messiah, and therefore God had to abandon them. Such an argument ignores the explicit and abundant testimony of the Gospels that from the beginning of His ministry until the end, enthusiastic crowds admired and followed Jesus (Luke 4:14, 15; 19:48; 21:38),[18] so much so that the leaders "feared the multitudes" and had every reason to believe that the whole population would turn to Jesus: "If we let Him alone like this, everyone will believe in Him" (John 11:48). Even Caiaphas, the high priest of that year, could argue that "it is expedient for us that one man should die for the people, and not that the whole nation should perish" (verse 50). The biblical author notes, significantly, that Caiaphas made his statement under prophetic inspiration (verse 51).

The rejection interpretation also overlooks the historical context and circumstances of the Crucifixion. The biblical evidence suggests that only a small group of Jews participated in the event (consider, for example, the restricted space of the Praetorium, where Jesus' trial was held) and that many of them had no idea of what they were doing (Luke 23:34). In addition, we must keep in mind His followers, who knew what was happening but kept silent (Matt. 26:69-74), as well as the Romans, who were the actual executors.[19] The rejection theory not only dismisses historical truth that involves Jews, "Christians," and also Romans, but also forfeits the theological truth that "the iniquity of us all" (Isa. 53:6) killed Him. So when John (1:11) says, "He came to His own, and His own did not receive Him" (another classic reference in the rejection theory), he does not refer to "His own" as exclusively Israel—the Jews—but rather the world, all humans in time and in space, all creation in a cosmic sense (verses 1-5, 10). And the Gospel explicitly states that "the *world [kosmos]* did not know Him" (verse 10).

### 4. THE CURSE

The small crowd of Jews gathered for Jesus' trial declared those fateful words "His blood be on us and on our children" (Matt. 27:25). The statement is an important element of the rejection theory, for it shifts the spurning of the Jews beyond the actual event of the Crucifixion down through the centuries that follow, including the Crusades, the Inquisition, the Holocaust, and forever. But the argument of the curse ignores not only the immediate context of the Gospel story, but also the general biblical context of curses and the biblical view of theodicy.

According to the testimony of Scripture, this statement of guilt and punishment came only from a small group of Jews under the initiative and pressure of the chief priests, who were ultimately responsible[20] for it (Matt. 27:20). The book of Acts confirms this version of the facts, since the chief priests, responding to Peter's testimony about Christ, allude to that curse upon themselves: "You . . . intend to bring this Man's blood upon us!" (Acts 5:28). Only the high priests were (or will be) affected by the curse they initiated, since only they were "politically" threatened by this Messiah, who was "to bring an end to the sacrifices" and thus the legitimacy of their leadership. The rest of the people, according to Jesus Himself, did not know what was happening. That is why Jesus Himself implored God's forgiveness: "Father, forgive them, for they do not know what they do" (Luke 23:34).[21] Too often we forget this final supplication when we refer to the curse on the Jews. And yet, which one of these two prayers was the more worthy to be heard and answered—the "prayer" of those few ignorant and deceived Jews, or the prayer of the Son of God on the cross?

In fact, the idea of a curse that pursues the Jews throughout the ages contradicts the biblical teaching of curses and calls into question the character of the historical God and His compassion: "The Lord is longsuffering and abundant in mercy, forgiving iniquity and transgression" (Num. 14:18). This does not mean that God does not take iniquity seriously or merely tolerates it: "He by no means clears the guilty, visiting the iniquity of the fathers on the children to the third and fourth generation" (verse 18). In other words, the curses of God do not go beyond the fourth generation at the most.[22] Yet the defenders of the rejection theory, more zealous than God Himself (and therefore replacing Him), have carried the curse into the gas chambers of Auschwitz.

The idea that the suffering of the Jews is evidence of the curse and of their sin contradicts the biblical view of theodicy, which is more nuanced and "human." Along with the curses found in the book of Deuteronomy that sketch the clear-cut framework of covenant—if you obey, you will be blessed and happy; if you disobey, you will be cursed and unhappy—the

Bible also contains the book of Job and the story of the Crucifixion in the New Testament. These examples alert us to any kind of theology that uses a person's suffering as proof of God's judgment and as evidence of guilt. Job's defense against his friends and Jesus' cry on the cross should help us understand that suffering, the Holocaust, AIDS, tragic accidents, and the crucifixion of Jesus are not necessarily proof that the victim has sinned. If the principle is true that sin leads to suffering and to God's reproach, the reverse is not automatically valid: the suffering of a person *does not* indicate that an individual has committed a crime and been rejected by God. The suffering of the Jews *does not* mean that they are guilty and divinely abandoned. Simply because the Jews were the victims of the Holocaust does not mean that they were under a curse because they had spurned Jesus. In fact, a good number of these Jews were also Christians, who had accepted Jesus in their hearts.[23] They were victimized, not "because of their beliefs, their politics, or their military or social threat, but simply because of who or what others *imagined* them to be."[24] In fact, the verdict of Jewish guilt as a result of their suffering is all the more suspect when urged by professed Christians who have perpetrated that very suffering. Others use it as a divine justification for their crime of indifference.[25] To evoke God in that context is indecent. As Jules Isaac states: "Human iniquity is enough; don't involve God in it!"[26]

## 5. TURNING TO THE GENTILES

The fact that Peter calls the Gentile Christians "a chosen generation, a royal priesthood, a holy nation" (1 Peter 2:9), language that Deuteronomy 7:6 applies to Israel, does not mean that Gentiles have replaced the other Israel, thereby implying the rejection of the latter. Peter is simply saying that such Gentiles are now a part of the chosen people. Belonging to the house of Israel, they are "a chosen generation" like and within, not instead of, Israel.

Similarly, Acts 13:46 (among other texts in the same book), which reports that Paul and Barnabas went to the Gentiles, does not imply that God had now rejected the Jews. Verses 43-45 clarify that in fact many of the Jews still received the gospel: "many of the Jews and devout proselytes" (verse 43), "almost the whole city" (verse 44), and "the multitudes" (verse 45). It is only a minority, called in verse 45 "the Jews,"[27] who, seeing "the multitudes, . . . were filled with envy; and . . . opposed the things spoken by Paul." In addition, the following chapters of Acts clearly show that Paul continued preaching to the Jews and with great success.[28]

## 6. THE "ISRAEL OF GOD"

The expression "Israel of God" appears in Galatians 6:16: "And as many as walk according to this rule, peace and mercy be upon them, and upon the Israel of God." Supersessionists have traditionally understood the expression "Israel of God" in this passage as referring to the Gentile Christians, implying that the Christian church had taken the place of the Jewish people as "the true spiritual Israel."[29] For dispensationalists or futurists (see Section II) the designation "Israel of God" describes those descendants of Abraham who have been converted to Christianity. This group bases their argument on the Greek conjunction *kai,* which they read in the sense of "and," implying two distinct peoples: the "Israel of God" (the Jews) and the church (those who "walk according to this rule").

However, neither of the above interpretations takes into consideration the context and syntax of the passage. I would like to suggest two alternative interpretations that support neither supersessionist nor dispensationalist theological presuppositions.

Richard Longenecker suggests that "Paul is using a self-designation of his Jewish-Christian opponents in Galatia."[30] These legalistic Christians were arguing that their strict observances to the law as a means for salvation would make them more fully "the Israel of God." The phrase itself is unique and does not appear elsewhere in the New Testament or in Hellenistic or rabbinic literature. One may postulate that these Judaizers created the expression as a part of their specific doctrine. Moreover, the unusual and somewhat illogical order "peace and mercy" betrays intentionality. Elsewhere in the New Testament when benedictions associate mercy with "peace," mercy is always the cause that precedes "peace."[31] It is also the case for the classic benediction "grace and peace,"[32] in which "grace" as the cause precedes "peace" as the result. Considering the syntax of this phrase, some interpreters have therefore suggested the following reading of Galatians 6:16: "Peace on those who follow this rule, and mercy on the Israel of God." According to this reading, the peace benediction is on behalf of the Gentile converts of Galatia who follow the rule of verse 15 as a result of having already experienced mercy. Ironically the additional mercy benediction is on the legalistic Judaizing Christians who are still in need of that mercy.[33]

Others, including Gerhard Hasel and Leonard Goppelt, interpret Galatians 6:16 in a second way. Observing that the *"kai* is contextually best understood to be explicative,"[34] this position applies "the eschatological people of God,"[35] or "the true, the eschatological, people of God"[36] to the "Israel of God." In this case the expression would then refer to the same entity as the "all Israel" of Romans 11:26 that includes both Jews and non-Jews (cf. 1 Peter 2:9, 10) and that is the same ideal Israel. The passage implies neither the church nor Israel as earthly political, religious, or cultural entities, but rather a people that exists in God's mind, the Israel who will ultimately inherit the heavenly kingdom.

Many other interpretations have been suggested: a believing Jewish remnant, a non-Judaizing group of Jewish Christians, or the church in the time of Paul. Scholars have not reached a definite consensus on this text. The variety of opinions and the exceptional use of the phrase "Israel of God" should warn us against building dogmatic theories based on the passage. The evidence is indeed too shaky to infer from it the idea of a new Israel replacing an old Israel rejected by God.

## 7. THE OLIVE TREE

Nowhere in the New Testament do we find the rejection of Israel. In fact, the only time the biblical text speaks about any rejection of Israel, it emphatically affirms that God has not rejected them. "Has God cast away His people?" (Rom. 11:1) Paul asks. His answer is clear and unambiguous: "Certainly not!" And his response "Certainly not!" is all the more significant as it occurs *after* the Crucifixion, even after the first "Jewish" resistance to the "Christian" proclamation.

No exegetical reason exists to believe that in Romans 11:3-6 Paul has in mind another spiritual Israel that is distinct from the "people" he just spoke about in Romans 10:21. Both Romans 10:21 and 11:2 employ the word "Israel" in negative terms. Israel is unfaithful. Yet Paul still refers to Israel as "His people."[37]

The danger Paul is addressing arises in large part out of the expulsion of Jews from Rome in A.D. 49, who now return after the death of Claudius I in A.D. 54. Many of those returning were Jewish Christians (such as Priscilla and Aquila), which may have caused friction between Gentiles and Jews. The greater vulnerability of these Jews on the one hand and the growing self-confidence of the Gentile Christians on the other could explain why Paul felt it necessary to warn his Gentile readers against any feelings of superiority and the supersessionist idea that they had replaced the Jews not only in political leadership but also theologically. Thus, according to Paul, Gentile Christians are still dependent upon the heritage stemming from Abraham through the Jews.[38] To prove his point that God has not rejected Israel[39] or replaced it with the Gentiles, Paul structures his discourse around three arguments:

*The argument of the Jewish Christians (Romans 11:1-10).* "For I also am an Israelite, of the seed of Abraham, of the tribe of Benjamin" (verse 1). Here Paul does not use a spiritual language, but refers to the concrete historical line of his genealogy. Even the reference to Elijah in verses 2-4 is not spiritual, but is also a personal appeal to his own ancestry (cf. Phil. 3:5), since Elijah was also a Benjamite (cf. 1 Chron. 8:27). "Here I am," he says to the Gentile Christians (Rom. 11:18) of that time, who were tempted by a version of the rejection–supersessionist theory.[40] The fact that Paul, a Jew, had received Christ in his life was clear evidence that God had not rejected His people, the Jewish people. That there were Jewish Christians was the clear sign that proved that God had not abandoned the Jewish people. "I know in my flesh," Paul argued, in the reality of my person and my existence, that God is still with my people. I am the confirmation, the verification, that what you say about my people—that they are cursed, rejected by God, deceitful, and all the portraits you make in your "teaching of contempt"—is not the truth. I am before you as a part of the remnant, visible evidence that God has not spurned His people.

The prophet Isaiah employed the same reasoning[41] when he referred to a remnant whose presence guaranteed the survival and selection of the chosen people: "Unless the Lord of hosts had left to us a very small remnant, we would have become like Sodom, we would have been made like Gomorrah" (Isa. 1:9). Note that the text does not imply that because of Israel's unfaithfulness the people were now rejected and replaced by a remnant. Here also the remnant serves as a sign (the historical evidence) that Israel remained God's people. The fact that there was a remnant in Israel kept God from destroying the people and turning them into Sodom and Gomorrah. Incidentally, Isaiah deliberately alludes to Sodom and Gomorrah in that context since the biblical record tells us that in their cases no remnant was even possible (Isa. 1:9; Gen. 18:32, 33).

In other words, if Paul refers to himself as a Christian, it is not to suggest the idea that a "spiritual" Israel is a "remnant" replacing an ethnic, physical Israel. The "remnant" remains a part of the ethnic Israel even though it is not all of Israel. And the fact that there is still a remnant in Israel, and "I am a part of this remnant," Paul declares, should tell you that your idea of rejection and replacement does not hold, and that God has not spurned His people.

*The argument of the "saved" Gentiles (Romans 11:11-25).* Even when the Jews "stumble," Paul comments, it aids the salvation of the Gentiles. The original Greek text does not use the word "fall" or "rejected," but "stumble," or "trespass" (*eptaisan, paraptomati,* from *ptaio*), implying that they are still standing and surviving. Paul says explicitly: "That they should fall? Certainly not!" (verse 11). Note that Paul uses the same "certainly not" (*me genoito*) as in verse 1, in both cases relating to the idea of Paul's "rejection" of the "fall" of Israel. But through their stumbling, he observes, "salvation has come to the Gentiles" (verse 11).

Paul's reference to the "stumbling" of some Jews, that is, their resistance to the gospel, should be understood in context. Paul responds to those Gentiles who boast of their superiority over the Jews, because, as Christians, they saw something that the Jews did not yet see. Even if the Jews stumble, Paul argues, this very stumbling is good for you, Gentiles. It is a blessing for you, for their being cut off allows you to be grafted. Here Paul brings out the full implication of God's purpose to bless the nations through the seed of Abraham. He interprets Genesis 12:3 ("In you [Abraham] all the families of the earth shall be blessed" *[nibrekhu]*) by playing on the word *brk* that Second Temple literature used with a secondary meaning of "engrafting." Paul's interpretation of the "engrafting" of the Gentiles is similar to that of R. Eleazar as reported in the Talmud: "What is meant by the text, 'In you all the families of the earth shall be blessed' (Gen. 12:3)? The *qadosh Barukh Hu* (the Holy Blessed Be He) said to Abraham, 'I have two goodly shoots [*brakhot;* blessings] to engraft [*lehabrikh;* make blessing] on you: Ruth the Moabitess and Naaman the Syrian. All the families of the earth, even the other families who live on the earth.'"[42] In other words, Paul tells the Gentiles, your blessing is not owing to your own merits (you are a wild olive and therefore unproductive), but is the result of your grafting to the good and productive olive tree.[43] So instead of capitalizing on the "fall" of the Jews, theorizing a theology of rejection and boasting about Gentile spiritual superiority, you should rejoice and be grateful and humble, because you owe them your salvation, even in their trespass. The point of Paul's argument is not so much the stumbling of those Jews as it is the arrogance and the boasting of the Gentiles. The apostle does not necessarily imply that he believes Israel as a people—all the Jews (or even the majority)—have stumbled. Paul speaks only of "some of the branches" (Rom. 11:17). Also the literary and thematic connection between verses 15 and 17 favors the interpretation that the "casting away" in verse 15 has the same application as verse 17, namely, only "some" of Israel.

"If their being cast away . . ." (verse 15).

"If some of the branches were broken off . . ." (verse 17).

It is noteworthy that the verb translated "cast away" (verse 15) is not the same word as that used in Romans 11:1, in which we have *apotheo*, meaning "reject" and implying a person as accusative (Acts 7:27; 13:46; 1 Tim. 1:19), while in Romans 11:15 we have *apoballo*, meaning "to throw off," "to let go," and implying an object as accusative (e.g., Mark 10:50). It is also interesting to note that the Septuagint text of Isaiah 1:30 employs the same Greek *apoballo* also in association with a tree.

And even when Paul speaks of this "rejection," it is not a natural part of his personal argument. He simply goes along with the argumentation of those Gentiles ("you will say" [Rom. 11:19]; "well said" [verse 20]) and returns it against them in a typically rabbinic fashion.

*The argument of the people of Israel (verses 25-36).* In Paul's

31

perspective, even if the Jews stumble and some natural branches have been cut out of the olive tree, their grafting back into their own olive tree is all the more expected and will work more naturally than the grafting in of the wild branches. He aims this observation against the Christian Gentiles who boasted about their superiority over the Jews who stumbled. Although you are saved, he says, and they are not, and although you now have something they do not have, remember that if salvation was made possible for you, the wild branches, it will be all the more possible (the rabbinic form of reasoning, *qal wahomer:* a fortiori)[44] for the Jews, the natural branches to be saved.

Paul focuses on Israel and draws from historical reality two reasons that God has not rejected His people. The first reason pertains to the roots of Israel and concerns their "election." Insisting on the fact that "they are beloved for the sake of the fathers" (Rom. 11:28), he bases his discourse on a rabbinic principle, *Zekhut Avot* ("merits of the fathers").[45] Not that Paul believed that the Jews will automatically be saved through the merits of their fathers. Rather, their election, not their salvation, still remains for the sake of their fathers. In the process he thus reaffirms the election despite their stumbling. Paul's sadness that not all the Jews are accepting Jesus does not keep him from recognizing them as chosen people (see Rom. 9:1-5).

The sorrow of Paul, as well as that of Jesus, who wept over Jerusalem (Luke 13:34), should not be used as an argument to support the rejection of Israel. Those sentiments and exhortations reveal the love and concern that both Paul and the Son of God have for Israel, who is still dear to their hearts.

The second reason pertains to the fruit of Israel (the Messiah Himself; see Rom. 9:5) and the branches that God will someday graft back onto the tree. It is from this perspective that the apostle directs the argument against the idea of Israel's rejection. Again using rabbinic reasoning (*qal wahomer:* a fortiori), Paul once more underlines the election of Israel. Even the branches that have been cut off keep their nature as an "olive tree." The natural branches did not lose their character as "chosen" branches. Paul still considered the Israelites who had not accepted Jesus to be the chosen people and thus deserving of respect because of their past election and the roots that carried them. They were also witnesses to the divine revelation (see verses 4, 5)—"for the gifts and the calling of God are irrevocable" (Rom. 11:29)—and the eschatological hope of the regrafted branches. Then, from within this eschatological perspective, Paul elaborates on the hope of their final salvation: "And so all Israel will be saved" (verse 26). This new eschatological context of salvation invests the entity of Israel with a new meaning. But even here Paul does not speak about a "spiritual" Israel—the Christians, the Jewish Christians, the Gentiles, or the church that would replace unfaithful Israel. Nor does he refer to Jewish Israel, either. But he sees beyond the present earthly realities and dreams of the "saved" Israel. This "new" Israel is a part of the "New Jerusalem"—the heavenly Israel, the 144,000 of Revelation 14:3, "who are redeemed from the earth." According to Paul, in this "Israel" will be found *all* the redeemed people. It is the same "all Israel" implied in Romans 9:6, which includes Jews (the natural branches [Rom. 11:24]) and Gentiles (the wild branches [verse 25]). The expression "all Israel," which is typically Deuteronomic in style, refers to the totality of the people just before their entry into the Promised Land (Deut. 34:12; cf. 27:9; 31:1, 7). It is a well-known idiom that has

Creation-apocalyptic overtones (Isa. 45:18, 24, 25; Dan. 9:7, 8; Lev. 16:21, 22; cf. Gen. 2:1-3) referring to the cosmic view of salvation.

## 8. THE 70-WEEKS PROPHECY

Daniel 9, although it is an Old Testament text, deals prophetically with New Testament events: the coming of the Messiah, the end of the Temple sacrifices, the destruction of Jerusalem, and the universalization of the covenant. Since it speaks about the crucifixion of Jesus, the destruction of Jerusalem, and the birth of Christianity, it has become a classic reference in the rejection-supersessionist theory as well as being a favorite text in Adventist apologetics.

*"Seventy weeks are determined for your people" (Dan. 9:24).* Many understand the passage to imply that God has given 70 weeks as the "last chance for Israel," their "test" or "probation," God's ultimatum for His chosen people. But this ignores the overall context and structure of the 70-weeks prophecy within Daniel 9 and the immediate syntactic construction of the sentence. The literary structure of the text suggests that the word "people" belongs to the same line as the Messiah.[46] In other words, the mention of the "people" by virtue of its literary association with Messiah carries a note of hope and salvation, for the Messiah will come *from this people* and *for this people.* Thus it is good news for the people, tidings of liberation and redemption rather than warnings of dead end and rejection. This perspective of hope fits the general theological context of a chapter that describes Daniel as hoping and praying to God for the salvation of His people. As a result, this prophecy comes as a positive response from God to Daniel's request (verse 21).

Also the construction of the passage suggests that the passive verb "determined" *(nechtak)* is to be connected to what follows: "to finish the transgression, to make an end of sins." The 70 weeks are "determined" on the people to "finish the transgression"[47] (note the same construction in the phrase "remember the Sabbath day, to keep it holy" [Ex. 20:8]).

*"To finish the transgression, to make an end of sins" (Dan. 9:24).* Some interpret this passage to mean that the people of Israel are now "determined" to put an end to sin. But such a reading is blasphemous, for only God can bring an end to sin. Others have understood the passage to mean the "consummation of sin," that is, "within this period the Jews would fill the cup of their iniquity." But such a meaning of the verb *kl'* is hardly justifiable in view of textual and linguistic considerations as well as the book's immediate and general context.[48] And even if there were still any doubt, the syntactical and literary structure definitely suggests another direction.

Indeed, the verb *nechtak* ("determined") should not be connected to "your people and your city," thereby making "your people" the subject of the verb "to finish the transgression." Such a construction would imply that the people would also be the subject of the other verbs, "to make reconciliation for iniquity, to bring in everlasting righteousness, to seal up vision and prophecy, and to anoint the Most Holy"(verse 24), words that can have only God as the subject. In fact, the technical passive form *nechtak* ("determined") suggests God as the subject, a form also called the "divine passive."[49] It is God who does the salvific operation. We should, therefore, read: "The 70 weeks [by God] have been determined . . . to make an end to the transgression." The association of three specific notions—atonement *(kpr),* anointing *(masach),* and Holy of Holies *(qodesh qodashim)*—implies that the subject is God or the Messiah. These three elements also appear in Exodus 29:36, 37, the only other biblical reference that combines all these notions and deals with the consecration of Aaron and his sons to the Israelite priesthood. The shared association between the two texts suggests that the 70-weeks prophecy is hinting at the consecration of a new high priesthood.

From the start, the 70-weeks prophecy conveys the ultimate goal, the raison d'être, of the 70-weeks period. The 70 weeks have not been "determined" *against* the Jews to mark their fate or imply the rejection of Israel. The purpose of the 70 weeks is, instead, the good news of the salvation of the Jews and of the world through the work of the new High Priest. This event, which took place in A.D. 31 as reported by Peter, describes Jesus as sitting at the right hand of the Father after His ascension (1 Peter 3:22). Further the event is confirmed in A.D. 34, precisely at the end of the 70 weeks, by Stephen, who saw at that very moment "the heavens opened and the Son of Man standing at the right hand of God!" (Acts 7:56). Note, incidentally, that both passages locate the Messiah "at the right hand of God," the very terms used in Psalm 110, which also foretells the installment of the Davidic Messiah, as "a priest forever according to the order of Melchizedek" (verse 4): "The Lord said to my Lord, 'Sit at My right hand'" (verse 1), and "The Lord is at Your right hand" (verse 5).

*"But not for Himself" (Dan. 9:26).* Rejectionists/supersessionists interpret this phrase to imply that God has abandoned Israel. This expression *eyn lo* (literally "no one for him") is, in fact, unusual. Normally the phrase appears with a complement object to express the benefit of a possession (see Isa. 55:1; Esther

2:7) or with a participle to indicate the consequences of an action (see Gen. 41:8; Lam. 1:2, 9, 17). The absence of both grammatical elements suggests that the phrase is a contracted form of a longer one. Since the only other occurrence of the phrase *eyn lo* in the book of Daniel is in the longer phrase *eyn 'ozer lo* of ("no one [helping] him" [Dan. 11:45]), we may infer that *eyn lo* is the contracted form of *eyn 'ozer lo*.

Now, considering the fact that the verb *'azar* ("help") implies God as the subject in Daniel 11:45 (see also Dan. 10:13) and that the Bible often uses the verb *'azar* to refer to God's salvific work (see 1 Chron. 12:18; 2 Chron. 18:31; 1 Sam. 7:12; Ps. 30:10, 11; 86:17; 118:13; 119:173; Isa. 41:14; 49:8), it is reasonable to conclude that the unusual expression *eyn lo* ("no one for him," meaning "no one [helping] him") may refer to God's total abandonment of the Messiah in the latter's death. Incidentally, it is interesting to note that Psalm 22:11 employs the phrase *eyn 'ozer* ("no one to help") to describe God's total withdrawal at the Messiah's death.[50]

*"He shall confirm a covenant" (Dan. 9:27).* Here the rejection/supersessionist theory argues that this verse teaches that the coming of the Messiah will be the occasion of a "new covenant" with a "new people," abrogating the old covenant and rejecting the old people. But in fact the Hebrew word *higbir* ("confirm," from the root *gbr*, denoting strength) suggests the idea of a confirmation, a strengthening, a refreshing of the already-existing covenant rather than its abrogation. Moreover, this covenant concerns the *rabbim* ("many"), a technical term that connotes the idea of universality.[51] It refers to "all the saved ones" (see Dan. 12:2; Isa. 53:12). This covenant is thus not only "strengthened" with "many" Jews, but also with "many"

Gentiles, something that will happen at the end of the final prophetic week (A.D. 34). An important event for human civilization and salvation, it is the year when the message of the God of Israel exploded beyond the borders of Palestine and reached out to the Gentiles (Acts 8). Not only is it the year of Paul's conversion and apostolic commission (Acts 9); it is also the year God poured His Holy Spirit on the "many," a crucial moment that fulfills Jesus' prophecy about the shift from the visible theocracy that climaxed in the Incarnation, to the invisible regime of the Spirit (John 16:7). This prophecy does not speak of the rejection of the Jews, but of the adoption of the Gentiles, who are not seen as replacing the Jews but as joining them (they are grafted into them).

It is interesting to note that the book of Daniel does contain the idea of replacement or supersessionist behavior, a key motif that the book always associates with the little horn or the king of the north (Dan. 7:25; 11:7, 20). This entity represents a supersessionist power that *claims* to have taken the place of Israel and of the Messiah Himself. The advocates of the supersessionist theory, indeed, find themselves in dubious company.

*"And the people of the prince . . . shall destroy the city and the sanctuary" (Dan. 9:26).* The supersessionist expositors have interpreted this line as declaring that it was the Jews who were the "real" agents of the destruction of Jerusalem. In this view the "people of the prince" *('am nagid)* are not the Romans but the Jewish people. Incidentally, a similar way of thinking was (and still is) used in classic anti-Semitic slogans and more recently in the vicious revisionist argument that seeks to blame the Jews and not the Nazis for the Holocaust. Yet this reading of the biblical text stumbles on serious historical and exegetical evidence.

1. The plain meaning of the text and its actual *historical* fulfillment contradict the argument. The Jewish people did not destroy the city but were themselves the victims of the destruction. The Roman Empire was the agent of this destruction, and, as such, the power intended in the prophetic oracle. It is not only unfair but also historically incorrect to blame the Jews for the destruction of Jerusalem simply because they revolted against Rome. To assert that if the Jews had not rebelled, the Roman army would never have intervened and Jerusalem would have been spared is only speculation. The outbreak of war in A.D. 66 that led to the destruction of Jerusalem by Titus in A.D. 70 was the *culmination* of a long series of conflicts that began with Pompey's conquest in 63 B.C. In fact, this string of abuses was such that it led the Roman historian Tacitus to blame the Roman procurators alone for the Jewish revolt: "The Jews' resistance lasted until Gessius Florus became procurator."[52] Even Flavius Josephus acknowledged that "Florus forced us [the Jews] to take war against the Romans."[53] No wonder that modern historian Emil Schürer concludes: "It may be thought, from the record of the Roman procurators to whom . . . public affairs in Palestine were entrusted, that they all, as if by secret arrangement, systematically and deliberately set out to drive the people to revolt."[54]

2. The reasoning that identifies the Jews as the subject of the verb "destroy" (Jerusalem) goes against Daniel's normal practice that explicitly denounces the actual political and physical agent of the destruction (Dan. 1:1; 2:37-44; 5:30, 31; 7:17-25; 8:20-22; 11:2-45).

3. The book of Daniel associates the phrase *'am nagid* ("people of the prince") with the verb *ba'* ("come"), a verb that

belongs to the book's military language and always describes the march of an army in an act of aggression. Chapter 11 uses this verb 17 times and every time with this particular connotation.[55]

4. It is also significant that the same verbal form *yashchit* ("destroy") in Daniel 9:26 is also used in Daniel 8:24, 25 with the little horn as its subject.[56]

5. Since the word *'am* ("people") is used here without a pronominal suffix, it cannot be "Israel." Whenever Daniel refers to the people of Israel, it is always with the pronominal suffix *'amkha* ("you people" [Dan. 9:15, 16, 19, 24; 10:14; 11:14; 12:1]) or *'ami* ("my people" [Dan. 9:20).[57]

6. The structure of the 70-weeks prophecy clearly places the verb *yashchit* in the section dealing with the city of Jerusalem with its keyword *chrts* (see section $B_2$ in the table on page 57) and does not allow, therefore, the association between *yashchit* and the thematic line of "Messiah," a connection that is implied if we interpret the "people" as the Jewish people (i.e., people of the Messiah) instead of the Romans.

7. Another implication of this observation is that the *nagid* ("prince") of Daniel 9:26 cannot be the same figure as the *nagid* qualifying the Messiah in verse 25. In fact, the second *nagid* stands against the first one—as his adversary and usurper. We find this interpretation of the word *nagid* further confirmed intertextually by Ezekiel 28:2, which applies the word *nagid* to the prince of Tyre, a personification of the cosmic power of usurpation (Satan). This oracle not only refers explicitly to our Daniel (Eze. 28:3),[58] but shares a significant number of keywords in common[59] with Daniel 9:24-27. It is also noteworthy that this passage is the only one in which Ezekiel uses the word *nagid* to refer to princes. Elsewhere he always employs the synonym *nasi'*[60] (e.g., Eze. 7:27;

12:10; 26:16; 27:21; 44:3). Such an exception must therefore be intentional. In it Ezekiel refers to another kind of prince and means to suggest here the same cosmic and usurping power (see Eze. 28:2, 5, 9, 17) as the *nagid* of Daniel 9:26 and the little horn of Daniel 7:8, 25 and especially Daniel 8:10-12, 25.

8. Note that an interpretation that brings along the second *nagid* against the saving power of the Messiah, the first *nagid* (Dan. 9:25, 26), is consistent with the great controversy pattern that runs through the whole book of Daniel. Indeed, all prophetic visions systematically bring out the same scenario of the two antagonistic powers. In Daniel 2 the kings of the earth (i.e., the iron mixed with the clay) stand against the stone and the heavenly mountain (verses 44, 45). In Daniel 7 the little horn stands against the Most High and the Son of man (verse 25). In Daniel 8, again the little horn stands against the Most High and the Prince of princes (verses 11, 25). In Daniel 10, human princes stand against Michael (verses 13, 20). In Daniel 11 the king of the north, followed by the king of the south, stands against the glorious holy mountain (verse 45). Thus, if we did not have the evil power opposing the Messiah in the vision of Daniel 9, it would be an unusual exception.

*Excursus: a rabbinic curse about Daniel.* We need to rectify a misconception (and a calumny) about a so-called rabbinic curse regarding the study of the 70-weeks prophecy. Some Christians have suggested that rabbis uttered a specific curse against those Jews who read the book of Daniel, thus seeking to discourage them from studying his prophecies and preventing them from concluding that Jesus was the Messiah. In fact, the curse simply attempts to prevent Jews from speculating about the time of the end and the coming of the Messiah lest they be discouraged if the Messiah did not come and thus err in disbelief. In order to appreciate and understand the true intention of this curse, the exact and entire text of the curse now follows:

"R. Sh'muel bar Nahmani said in the name of R. Yohanan: 'May the bones of those who calculate the [messianic] end be blown away! As soon as the time [calculated by them] arrives and the Messiah does not come, they say: "He will no longer come at all." Rather, wait for him, for it is said, *Though he tarry, wait for him* (Hab. 2:3).' " [61]

---

[1] See especially Bultmann's Theory of Scheitern in Claus Westermann, *Essays on Old Testament Hermeneutics,* ed. James Luther Mays (Richmond, Va.: John Knox Press, 1963), p. 73.

[2] See Jules Isaac, *The Teaching of Contempt: Christian Roots of Anti-Semitism,* trans. Helen Weaver (New York: Holt, Rinehart and Winston, 1964); Clark M. Williamson, *Has God Rejected His People? Anti-Judaism in the Christian Church* (Nashville: Abingdon, 1982), p. 105.

[3] For the history of the supersessionist theory, see John T. Pawlikowski, *Jesus and the Theology of Israel* (Wilmington, Del.: Michael Glazier, Inc., 1989), pp. 10, 11; cf. Jacques B. Doukhan, *Israel and the Church: Two Voices for the Same God* (Peabody, Mass.: Hendrickson Publishers, 2002), pp. 55-72.

[4] See Franklin H. Littell's oft-cited assertion that "the cornerstone of Christian Antisemitism is the superseding or displacement myth, which already rings with the genocidal note" (*The Crucifixion of the Jews: The Failure of Christians to Understand the Jewish Experience* [Macon, Ga.: Mercer University Press, 1986], p. 2). See also Darrell J. Fasching's definition of the doctrine of "supersession": "This can be simply defined as the belief that Christians have replaced Jews as God's chosen people, therefore they are the true Jews. It follows that Jews really have no right to continue existing. This is 'spiritual genocide'—the act of defining a people out of existence by appropriating their spiritual identity for one's own. It is this act which sets the stage and creates the precedents for the secular pseudoreligious program of physical genocide against the Jews by the Nazis. Words do indeed have the power to kill" (*The Jewish*

*People in Christian Preaching,* ed. Darrell J. Fasching [New York: E. Mellen Press, 1984], p. x).

[5] Some are more imaginative and start even earlier with the patriarchs by referring to the deceitful behavior of Abraham, Isaac, and Jacob. An interesting case is Jacob, who became Israel and embodied in himself the supersessionist thesis: spiritual Israel replaced Jacob the carnal deceiver. Such reasoning overlooks the fact that Scripture continues to use the name Jacob after this event, and it still receives positive spiritual meaning (Gen. 46:2, 5; 48:2; Num. 23:23; Isa. 48:20; Jer. 30:7; Eze. 28:25; etc.).

[6] See Ellen White's comments on these events: "Yet though they [the Israelites] were carried as captives to Babylon, God did not forsake them. He sent His prophets to them" (*Prophets and Kings* [Mountain View, Calif.: Pacific Press Pub. Assn., 1943], p. 582).

[7] John Bright, *The Kingdom of God: The Biblical Concept and Its Meaning for the Church* (Nashville: Abingdon-Cokesbury Press, 1953), p. 18.

[8] Of the 15 occurrences of the word "nation" *(ethnos)* in the book of Matthew, seven refer only to the Gentiles (Matt. 4:15; 6:32; 10:5, 18; 12:18, 21; 20:19).

[9] See Ellen G. White, *The Desire of Ages* (Mountain View, Calif.: Pacific Press Pub. Assn., 1898), p. 232.

[10] See John 19:39; Acts 5:34-40; 6:7.

[11] See Ellen G. White's comments on this parable where she also identifies the husbandmen of the vineyard as the "Jewish rulers" in contradistinction to the people (*Christ's Object Lessons* [Washington, D.C.: Review and Herald Pub. Assn., 1900], pp. 293, 294; *Review and Herald,* Feb. 18, 1890).

[12] *Jewish Antiquities* 28. 8.

[13] See Joseph Klausner, *Jesus of Nazareth: His Life, Times, and Teaching,* trans. Herbert Danby (New York: Macmillan Co., 1929), p. 357.

[14] G. Vermes, *The Dead Sea Scrolls in English,* 3rd ed. (New York: Penguin Books, 1987), p. 30.

[15] See Ellen White: "The Romans claimed the right of appointing and removing the high priest, and the office was often secured by fraud, bribery, and even murder. Thus the priesthood became more and more corrupt. Yet the priests still possessed great power, and they employed it for selfish and mercenary ends. The people were subjected to their merciless demands, and were also heavily taxed by the Romans. This state of affairs caused widespread discontent. Popular outbreaks were frequent. Greed and violence, distrust and spiritual apathy, were eating out the very heart of the nation" (*The Desire of Ages,* p. 30).

[16] On the concept of "corporate personality," see H. Wheeler Robinson, *The Christian Doctrine of Man* (Edinburgh: T. & T. Clark, 1911); cf. Joshua R.

Porter (who argues against the concept of corporate personality in the legal sphere of the Old Testament), "The Legal Aspects of the Concept of 'Corporate Personality' in the Old Testament," *Vetus Testamentum* 15, no. 3 (July 1965): 379, n. 5.

[17] W. D. Davies and Dale C. Allison, Jr., *Matthew,* International Critical Commentary (Edinburg: T. & T. Clark, 1997), vol. 3, p. 318; cf. Léon Poliakov, *The History of Anti-Semitism: From the Time of Christ to the Court Jews,* trans. Richard Howard (New York: Vanguard Press, 1965), vol. 1, pp. 29, 30.

[18] Jules Isaac, *Jesus and Israel,* ed., and with a foreword, by Claire Huchet Bishop, trans. Sally Gran (New York: Holt, Rinehart and Winston, 1971). Cf. Ellen G. White: "As Jesus traveled through Galilee, teaching and healing, multitudes flocked to Him from the cities and villages. Many came even from Judea and the adjoining provinces. Often He was obliged to hide Himself from the people. The enthusiasm ran so high that it was necessary to take precautions lest the Roman authorities should be aroused to fear an insurrection. Never before had there been such a period as this for the world. Heaven was brought down to men. Hungering and thirsting souls that had waited long for the redemption of Israel now feasted upon the grace of a merciful Saviour" (*The Desire of Ages,* p. 232).

[19] See Jacques Doukhan, *Drinking at the Sources: An Appeal to the Jew and the Christian to Note Their Common Beginnings,* trans. Walter R. Beach and Robert M. Johnston (Mountain View, Calif.: Pacific Press Pub. Assn., 1981), pp. 89-91.

[20] See also Ellen White, who specifically identifies the "priests and rulers" as those who rejected the Savior (*The Desire of Ages,* pp. 618, 619).

[21] Note that Jesus' prayer included not only the multitude of Jews who were attending the event, some of them even lamenting about it (verse 27), but also the two criminals (verse 32) and even the soldiers who divided His garments (verse 34).

[22] Speaking about the sin of the "Jewish rulers" who rejected Jesus, Ellen White warns, however: "The children were not condemned for the sins of the parents" (*The Great Controversy* [Mountain View, Calif.: Pacific Press Pub. Assn., 1911], p. 28).

[23] See Johanna-Ruth Dobschiner, *Selected to Live* (Old Tappan, N.J.: F. H. Revell Co., 1973); Rose Warmer and Myrna Grant, *The Journey: The Story of Rose Warmer's Triumphant Discovery* (Wheaton, Ill.: Tyndale House Publishers, 1978); etc.

[24] Rabbi Lester Bronstein, "Belief in the Human Spirit," in *Sacred Intentions,* eds. Kerry M. Olitzky and Lori Forman (Woodstock, Vt.: Jewish Lights Publishing, 1999), p. 137. (Italics supplied.)

[25] As Ellen White put it: "The heathen and those called Christians alike have been their foes. Those professed Christians, in their zeal for Christ,

whom the Jews crucified, thought that the more suffering they could bring upon them, the better would God be pleased" (*Early Writings* [Washington, D.C.: Review and Herald Pub. Assn., 1882], pp. 212, 213).

[26] Jules Isaac, *Genèse de l'Antisémitisme* (Paris: Calmann-Lévy, 1956), p. 172. Author's translation.

[27] On the use of the word "Jews" in the New Testament, see *Explorations* 9, no. 2 (1995).

[28] See Acts 14:1, 4; 17:1-5; 19:19-21; 28:17, 22, 24, 31.

[29] See Justin Martyr *Dialogue* 11. 5; cf. John Chrysostom, *Commentary on the Epistle to the Galatians and Homilies on the Epistle to the Ephesians* (Oxford: Parker, 1840).

[30] Richard N. Longenecker, *Galatians, Word Biblical Commentary* (Dallas: Word Books, 1990), vol. 41, p. 298.

[31] See 1 Tim. 1:2; 2 Tim. 1:2; Jude 2; etc.

[32] See Rom. 1:7; 1 Cor. 1:3; 2 Cor. 1:2; Gal. 1:3; Eph. 1:2; etc.

[33] Peter Richardson, *Israel in the Apostolic Church,* Society for New Testament Studies monograph series, no. 10 (London: Cambridge University Press, 1969), pp. 74-84.

[34] Gerhard F. Hasel, "Israel in Bible Prophecy" (unpublished paper, n.d.), p. 12.

[35] Leonhard Goppelt, *Theology of the New Testament,* ed. Jürgen Roloff, trans. John E. Alsup (Grand Rapids: Eerdmans, 1982), vol. 2, p. 145.

[36] Werner G. Kümmel, *The Theology of the New Testament According to Its Major Witnesses: Jesus—Paul—John,* trans. John E. Steely (Nashville: Abingdon Press, 1973), p. 211.

[37] Commenting on this passage, Ellen White observes that "even though Israel rejected His Son, God did not reject them" (*The Acts of the Apostles* [Mountain View, Calif.: Pacific Press Pub. Assn., 1911], p. 375). It is clear for Ellen White that Paul's words "His people" apply to the unfaithful Israel, the people she just referred to as "disobedient" (quoting Rom. 10:21 and Isa. 65:2), and not to an ideal remnant.

[38] See James D. G. Dunn, *Romans, Word Biblical Commentary* (Dallas: Word Books, 1988), vol. 38A, p. liii, and vol. 38B, p. 662.

[39] Paul's position in Romans 11 is consistent with the entire argument of Romans that presupposes the faithfulness of God to His people (see Rom. 1:16; 3:1-8); see Cristina Grenholm and Daniel Patte, eds., *Reading Israel in Romans: Legitimacy and Plausibility of Divergent Interpretations* (Harrisburg, Pa.: Trinity Press International, 2000), pp. 206-208.

[40] See William S. Campbell's comment on that passage: "Perhaps Paul encountered here for the first time a supersessionist form of Christianity that his own mission, at least as it was reported, had helped to produce" (Grenholm and Patte, p. 206). This is not, however, evidence of Gentile anti-Semitism

(see Paul S. Minear, *The Obedience of Faith: The Purposes of Paul in the Epistle to the Romans* [London: SCM, 1971], p. 79). Indeed, the idea of a Gentile anti-Semitism to support the Christian myth of an eternal anti-Semitism does not hold in the face of historical reality (see Isaac, *Genèse de l'Antisémitisme*). Also Christianity was not yet clearly distinct from Judaism. The Gentile Christians were, therefore, recruited among the Gentiles already attracted to Judaism (the "God-fearing" proselytes).

[41] The texts of Isaiah are very much in Paul's mind and are often quoted by him (see Rom. 10:21; 11:8, 26, 27, 34).

[42] Yebamoth 63a.

[43] On the image of the olive tree representing Israel both in the Bible and in Jewish tradition, see Jer. 11:16; Ps. 52:8; Menahoth 53b; Pesikta de-Rab Kahana 21.4.

[44] Sanhedrin 6:5; cf. Genesis Rabbah 92:7. For Paul's use of this classic hermeneutic formula, see also Rom. 5:15, 17; 11:12, 15.

[45] Shabbath 55a.

[46] See Jacques Doukhan, "The Seventy Weeks of Daniel 9: An Exegetical Study," *Andrews University Seminary Studies* 17, no. 1 (1979): 12.

[47] The preposition "to" is a *lamed* of purpose.

[48] The word *klh,* which means "cease," "come to an end" (see Ludwig Köhler and Walter Baumgartner, *The Hebrew and Aramaic Lexicon of the Old Testament* [New York: E. J. Brill, 1995), pp. 476, 477), is preferable over *kl'* ("consummate," "fill up"); see *BHS* Apparatus, ad loc. This occurrence of *kl'* is here unique in the book of Daniel which uses instead only the related root *klh* (9:27; 11:16, 36; 12:7). Also, the association with sin is attested only with *klh* and not with *kl'*.

[49] Joachim Jeremias, *New Testament Theology: The Proclamation of Jesus* (New York: Scribner, 1971), p. 13, coined the expression "passivum divinum."

[50] Compare also with the expression *eyn matsil miyado* (literally "no one saving from His hand" in Daniel 8:4, 8); cf. Doukhan, "The Seventy Weeks of Daniel 9," pp. 18, 19.

[51] See Doukhan, "The Seventy Weeks of Daniel 9," p. 13, n. 8.

[52] Tacitus *Histories* 5. 10. 1.

[53] *Jewish Antiquities* 20. 257.

[54] Emil Schürer, *The History of the Jewish People in the Age of Jesus Christ (175 B.C.-A.D. 135),* trans. T. A. Burkill et al., rev. and ed. Geza Vermes and Fergus Millar (Edinburgh: T. & T. Clark, 1973), vol. 1, p. 455.

[55] See especially the same form *habba'* in Daniel 11:16, which has the "king of the North" as a subject, who "shall stand in the Glorious Land with destruction in his power" (note the same associations with *klh* and in verse 12 with *hashchit*).

[56] As for the Hiphil (causative) form of *yashchit,* it does not imply a particular intention to suggest that the Jews "caused" to destroy the city of Jerusalem. The verb *shcht* never occurs in the Paal and is used in the Bible primarily in the Hiphil form with the direct meaning of "destroy," *always* implying the actual subject of the verb as the direct physical agent of destruction (in the book of Daniel, see, for instance, Dan. 8:24, 25 and Dan. 11:12, already mentioned). When it occurs (more rarely) in the Piel, Niphal, and Hophal, "there is no discernible difference." See R. Laird Harris, Gleason L. Archer, Jr., Bruce K. Waltke, eds., "*Shachat,* destroy, corrupt," in *Theological Wordbook of the Old Testament* (Chicago: Moody Press, 1981), vol. 2, p. 917. Note that the same form is attested in Egyptian language: the word *ski,* meaning "to destroy, annihilate," is also in the causative form, without implying a causative intention.

[57] Cf. Martin Pröbstle, "A Text-oriented Study of Daniel 8:9-14" (Ph.D. diss., Andrews University, forthcoming).

[58] For a discussion about the name Daniel in this passage, see Jacques Doukhan, *Daniel: The Vision of the End,* 2nd ed., rev. (Berrien Springs, Mich.: Andrews University Press, 1989), p. 121, n. 20.

[59] *Shachat,* "destruction" (Eze. 28:8, 17); *chtm,* "seal" (verse 12); *mshch,* "anoint" (verse 14); *qdsh* (verses 14, 16); *miqdash,* "sanctuary" (verse 18); *shmm,* "desolate" (verse 19); *'awon* (verse 18).

[60] Most of the occurrences of the word *nasi'* appear in Ezekiel.

[61] B. Sanhedrin 97b.

# The Dispensationalist Theory

Dispensationalism originated among the Plymouth Brethren of England in the early 1830s. The father of dispensationalism, John Nelson Darby (1800-1882), was one of the chief founders of the Plymouth Brethren movement, which arose in reaction against the formalism of the Church of England. Dispensationalist theology centers upon the concept that salvation history from Creation to God's kingdom divides into several "economies," or "dispensations," that imply different revelations and conditions by which God will test humanity. The number of dispensations varies depending on the theologian: seven for Darby; eight, 10, or even 12 for others; and three for contemporary dispensationalist Charles Ryrie. These include the old dispensation under the law of Moses, the present under grace, and the future during the millennium.

Popular prophetic meetings (i.e., the Niagara Bible Conferences), the broad diffusion of the Scofield annotated Bible, the impact of such media evangelists as Pat Robertson and Hal Lindsey, and such books and films as the *Left Behind* series have led to a wide acceptance of dispensationalism in the United States.

In this book we will not enter into all the debates about the dispensationalist theory, but we will discuss it insofar as it relates to "Israel," a central theme in the dispensationalist system.

The dispensationalist theory of Israel advocates that since the Jews rejected Jesus as Messiah, the fulfillment of the earthly kingdom that God had initially promised to them He postponed to the end of time. Instead He established the "mystery" form of the kingdom—the church—as a "parenthesis" that will last until the end. Christ will come invisibly to take the Christians to heaven (the rapture), where they will celebrate the "marriage feast with the Lamb" for a period of seven years. During the seven years, while the church remains in heaven, God's program will resume on earth for the Jews. The antichrist will reign and will sign a covenant with Israel, but will then turn around and oppress them during the last three and a half years (the tribulation). At the end of the seven-year period Christ will visibly return in glory, and all the Jews then alive will recognize Him as Messiah. Christ will save them from the antichrist and destroy His enemies at the battle of Armageddon. Then He will set up His Davidic throne in Jerusalem; the Temple will be rebuilt there (on Mount Zion), and sacrifices (for sins) will be offered. There He will reign over the Jews (the natural citizens) and many Gentiles (the adopted citizens) for 1,000 years. After the millennium Christ will destroy His last enemies, Satan and his followers. Concluding the final judgment, He will establish the new heavens and new earth, where Israel and the redeemed Gentiles will enjoy eternity, still and forever distinct from each other.

To support their theory and the whole scenario that it implies, dispensationalist theologians rely on the theological principle of the absolute distinction between the different dispensations, especially between that of Israel and the church. They also depend on a literal interpretation of key prophetic texts, such as the return prophecies of Isaiah, Jeremiah, and Ezekiel, the 70-weeks prophecy of Daniel, and the prophecy of the salvation of Israel found in Romans 11.

## 1. ISRAEL AND THE CHURCH

Dispensationalist theory starts with the premise that the Jews have rejected Jesus and thus upset God's original plan as outlined in the Scriptures. Thus God had to postpone the theocratic kingdom promised in the Old Testament until the end and then establish the church, something not predicted in the Hebrew Scriptures. In this view the New Testament functions as a kind of plan B, put into effect because of the failure of the Old Testament's plan A. For the dispensationalist the Old Testament is the book of Israel, the book of the earthly kingdom and of the law, while the New Testament is the book of grace and the church. As a result, we find two peoples absolutely separated from each other: the one natural and earthly; the other spiritual and heavenly.

In fact, dispensational theology inherited this view from traditional continental Protestantism in which the same Marcionite paradigm opposed law, the Old Testament, and earthly "carnal" Israel (the Jews). Instead it favored grace, the New Testament, and "spiritual" Israel (the church). But this "new" system[1] no longer describes the contrast between the two economies in supersessionist terms. Instead God gave the law for the Jews and grace for the Christians. And each one is responsible before God within their particular dispensation.

The first criticism we can make against dispensationalism

concerns the method itself. The distinctions between the various dispensations are often artificial and quite arbitrary. Frequently they overlap, for what characterizes one dispensation will also appear in another, and even the boundaries between them are unclear and often vary, depending on the great variety of dispensationalist positions.

This systematic classification into specific dispensations contradicts the Hebrew/biblical view of revelation. It not only breaks the unity of the Scriptures by setting the New Testament in opposition to the Old Testament, but also does not conform to God's revelation of Himself in the Bible. God certainly did not reveal Himself through elaborate theological systems or philosophical categories. The God of Abraham, Isaac, and Jacob, as well as the God of Paul, John, and Peter, has chosen to reveal Himself to humanity through history. The events of Creation, the Exodus, the giving of the law at Sinai, and the return from the Exile are examples. In addition, the person of Jesus Christ—His supernatural birth, extraordinary life, and resurrection—all carry theological lessons of God's revelation. Within the biblical perspective, theology derives from events, not the other way around. This principle of Hebrew thinking[2] is important, for it allows revelation to be universal, thus transcending various cultures. More important, it prevents human extrapolation about God that may lead us astray.

We see this last risk perfectly illustrated in dispensationalist theology, in which the preconceived dualistic/Marcionite views that pit the law of the Old Testament against the grace of the New Testament, and flesh against Spirit have prevailed over the actual truth of the Bible. Indeed, grace itself appears in the Old Testament (Ps. 31:16; Hosea 2:19), and the New Testament promotes law (Rom. 7:22-25; James 2:10). The Old Testament presents the same ideal of internalization of the law, along with prophetic calls for a circumcision of the heart, that the New Testament does (Deut. 6:4-6; cf. Jer. 9:25, 26; Matt. 5:21, 22, 27, 28; Rom. 2:29). Jesus and His disciples never intended to create a new dispensation, much less a new religion. The affirmation of Jesus as the Messiah did not imply another dispensation distinct from the Old Testament and the law: "Do not think that I came to destroy the Law or the Prophets," says Jesus. "I did not come to destroy but to fulfill" (Matt. 5:17). The Greek word *plerosai* means literally "to fill to the full." Instead of implying the annulment of the law, Jesus testified that He would "uphold" the law and make it blossom and mature. Later Paul argued the same point: "Do we then make void the law through faith? Certainly not! On the contrary, we establish the law" (Rom 3:31). Even when Gentiles decided to join the Christian community, they submitted to the law. The passionate discussions reported in Acts 15 clearly testify to the importance of the law in their theological thinking. Even the conclusion of the debate, which might at first glance seem to suggest a liberation from the law, still remains within traditional Judaism. We find similar discussions among the rabbis, who adopted the same legal measures for Gentiles wanting to join the Jewish community.[3]

Along the same lines, early Christians understood the coming of Jesus the Messiah within the context of Old Testament prophecies, an interpretation that incidentally contradicts the dispensationalist presupposition that the Old Testament has no connection with the New Testament. The first Christians regarded the First Advent as the fulfillment of Old Testament prophecy. In fact, Jewish Christians used messianic prophecies as their main argument to prove to other Jews that Jesus was the Jewish Messiah promised in the Hebrew Scriptures. For a Jew to become a Christian did not imply rejection or ignorance of the Old Testament. On the contrary, it was on the basis of the Old Testament that as a Jew someone could recognize Jesus as the Messiah.

Early Christianity remained within the confines of Israel, even after others began calling them "Christians" (Acts 11:26), a name that they did not choose for themselves. This designation seems to have come from outside, bestowed on them by pagan Greeks or Romans, perhaps as a derogatory nickname. The Christians preferred to use other names for themselves, such as "disciples," "brothers," or "saints." The non-Christian Jews used the Hebrew name *Notzrim,* or Nazarenes (from Nazareth), to designate the early Christians, whom they considered to be a Jewish sect (Acts 24:5). It is only much later, around the fourth century, after the Jewish-Christian separation, that the word *minim* ("heretics") came to be associated with the word *notzrim* ("Christian") in a curse intended to distinguish Christians from Jews.[4] The history of early Christianity contradicts, therefore, the dispensationalist claim of the necessary distinction between Israel and the church. Only later, through political turmoil and at the expense of theological compromise, did the church become a distinct entity apart from Israel.

This distinction, which resulted from the church's rejection of its Jewish roots, has become in dispensationalism a theological doctrine with some clear racist overtones. It regards Israel and the church as two different peoples, with no theological or ethnic connection whatsoever. But such teaching stands in flagrant contradiction to the testimony of the Old Testament Scriptures, which describes the people of Israel as a "mixed multitude" (Ex. 12:38) and views eschatological Israel as an open community that will ultimately join "many" peoples from all nations (Isa. 56:5, 6). To be a part of physical Israel in the Old Testament meant simply recognizing the God of Israel as one's personal God.

Dispensationalist teaching also ignores the New Testament principle that through Christ the Gentiles are no longer separated and distinct from the Jews, for they have become a part of Israel not just "spiritually" but also historically and physically. As Paul states in Ephesians 2:12-15, the Gentile who was once "alien," "far off," is now "brought near by the blood of Christ," for the wall that separated Jew and Gentile has now been broken down (see also Gal. 3:28, 29). The dispensationalist dichotomy between Israel and the church and what these entities represent—namely, law and grace, Old Testament and New Testament—therefore blatantly contradicts the historical reality of Israel in the Old Testament, or the early church in the New Testament, as well as the theological teaching of all Scripture.

## 2. THE SEVENTIETH "SEVEN"

Another implication of the Jewish rejection of Jesus paradoxically appears in the dispensationalists' prophetic recognition of the modern state of Israel. Dispensationalists argue that since the Jews rejected Jesus, God tabled His initial plan to give them the promised earthly kingdom until the time of the end, when Israel will again play a prophetic role. This last chapter of Israel's history they see as prophetically foreordained in the 70-weeks prophecy of Daniel 9:24-27, more precisely in verse 27, which deals with the seventieth seven, the last week of that prophetic period. Such dispensationalist interpretation separates this last week from the previous 69 weeks and postpones it until the end-times. Immediately after the rapture, according to the dispensationlist scenario, the events of this last week will take place on earth, while the saved Christians are in heaven:

1. At the beginning of the week the antichrist will enforce a covenant with Israel.

2. In the middle of the week the antichrist will cancel the covenant and start the oppression of Israel, the tribulation that will last until the end of the seventieth week.

The whole theory builds on a special exegesis of Daniel 9:27: "Then he shall confirm a covenant with many for one week." For dispensationalists the pronoun "he" refers to "the prince" of verse 26, identified with the antichrist or the little horn of Daniel 7, who will make a covenant with Israel at the end of time. However, this division of the passage that separates the last week from the others and makes the prince of Daniel 9:26 the subject of the covenant is neither supported by the overall structure of the passage nor by the lexical/theological connection between verses 26 and 27. The literary structure of the prophetic text (see below) displays a back-and-forth movement between two themes, that of the Messiah ($A_1$, $A_2$, $A_3$) and that of Jerusalem ($B_1$, $B_2$, $B_3$). Each theme is systematically associated with a common keyword. The three passages dealing with Jerusalem ($B_1$, $B_2$, $B_3$) have the keyword *chrts* ("determine, cut") in common, whereas the three passages dealing with the Messiah ($A_1$, $A_2$, $A_3$) refer regularly to a time expressed in terms of "weeks" *(shavu').*

"From the going forth of the command to restore and build Jerusalem" (verse 25).[5]

| A₁ **The Coming of the Messiah** "until the Messiah the Prince, there shall be seven *weeks (shavu')* and sixty-two weeks" (verse 25). | B₁ **Construction of the City** "the street shall be built again, and the wall [cut] *(chrts)* even in troublesome times" (verse 25). |
| --- | --- |
| A₂ **Death of the Messiah** "And after the sixty-two *weeks (shavu')* Messiah shall be cut off, but not for Himself" (verse 26). | B₂ **Destruction of the City** "And the people of the prince who is to come shall destroy the city and the sanctuary. The end of it shall be with a flood, and till the end of the war desolations are determined *(chrts)*" (verse 26). |
| A₃ **Covenant of the Messiah** "Then he shall confirm a covenant with many for one *week (shavu');* but in the middle of the week He shall bring an end to sacrifice and offering" (verse 27). | B₃ **Desolation of the City** "And on the wing of abominations shall come one who makes desolate, even until the consummation, which is determined *(chrts)* is poured out on the desolator" (verse 27).[6] |

In the flow of the prophetic text the two themes of the Messiah and Jerusalem appear alternately, giving this section its interwoven construction:

A₁ (verse 25) Messiah

B₁ (verse 25) Jerusalem

A₂ (verse 26) Messiah

B₂ (verse 26) Jerusalem

A₃ (verse 27) Messiah (here implied)

B₃ (verse 27) Jerusalem

The literary structure of the prophetic text leads to the following observations regarding the interpretation of the covenant in verse 27 (A₃):

1. Since the "covenant" in A$_3$ (verse 27) is associated with the keyword *shavu'* ("week"), which is regularly linked with the Messiah, it follows that this covenant should be related to the Messiah.

2. The alternating construction (Messiah-Jerusalem-Messiah-Jerusalem-Messiah-Jerusalem) confirms the implied presence of the Messiah in A$_3$.

The dispensationalist interpretation that relates the covenant to the prince, or antichrist, of verse 26 contradicts the literary structure of this phrase that suggests that it is the Messiah who is the agent of the covenant and not the prince.

Lexical and theological associations support the evidence of the literary structure. The word *krt* ("cut off"), which describes the death of the Messiah (verse 26), is the technical term normally linked with the covenant *(berit)*. Most of the occurrences of *krt* (130 times) appear in relation to the word *berit*.[7] The Hebrew text always describes the covenant as being cut off *(krt),* again confirming that the covenant *(berit)* discussed in verse 27 is related to the *krt* that describes the death of the Messiah in verse 26. If so, it identifies the death of the Messiah as a Levitical sacrifice through which the covenant is cut off. The cultic sacrificial language of the 70-weeks prophecy (e.g., "transgression," "sin," "atonement," "sacrifice and offering") further supports this interpretation. The covenant is of a cultic nature that relates to the sacrificial death of the Messiah and therefore has nothing to do with the dispensationalist view of a political covenant between the antichrist and the Jewish people.

The Hebrew verb *higbir* ("confirm" in NKJV) does not imply, as Joyce Baldwin argues, the idea of "forcing an agreement by means of superior strength."[8] Dispensationalists defend such an interpretation[9] to support their prophetic scenario that the antichrist will impose his covenant upon the Jews. The Hiphil form of the verb *gbr* ("strong") suggests instead a process that strengthens the covenant itself rather than its actual enforcement. Indeed, the form implies that the strengthening is in the covenant rather than in the agent of the covenant. The use of this form does not allow for the idea of a covenant made for the first time, but suggests instead that this covenant is rendered stronger, thus implying that it was already in existence. It is also significant that the only other biblical occurrence of this verb form of *higbir* occurs in Psalm 12:4, which associates the verb with the verb *gdl* ("great") in relation to the tongue that "speaks proud [great] things" (Ps. 12:3). The covenant is made stronger or greater, an idea confirmed by the object of this covenant, the "many" *(rabbim),* which connotes universality and implies a covenant broadened beyond the borders of Israel to embrace the nations. Interestingly, Isaiah 53, in which the suffering servant "shall justify many" (verse 11), also uses the same word, *rabbim.* The universal intention of this *berit* ("covenant") also appears in the syntax of the word that occurs here without the article ("the") as "Messiah" in Daniel 9:26. Indeed, the omission of the article is a stylistic device employed in the context of the whole text of the 70-weeks prophecy to express the universalistic intentions of that prophecy.[10]

It is also significant that the vision links this covenant not only with the death of the Messiah but also with the end of "sacrifice and offering" and is situated in time during "the middle of the week" (verse 27), the exact moment Christ died on the cross (A.D. 31). The prophecy portrays the death of the

Messiah as an atoning sacrifice, and, responding to the basic theological intention of the 70-weeks prophecy, it is designed "to make reconciliation ["atonement," *kpr*] for iniquity" (verse 24). This ultimate sacrifice will fulfill the prophecy symbolized by the sacrificial system. Antitype will meet type, and thus "seal up vision and prophecy" (verse 24). The Epistle to the Hebrews explains this process when it interprets the law of sacrifices as "a shadow of the good things to come" (Heb. 10:1) and declares that Christ "has appeared to put away sin by the sacrifice of Himself" (Heb. 9:26). For the author of the Epistle to the Hebrews the lesson of this event is clear: The sacrifice of Christ has made the animal sacrifices of the Levitical system obsolete. "He takes away the first that He may establish the second" (Heb. 10:9). And therefore, as far as we are concerned, we are now "sanctified through the offering of the body of Jesus Christ once for all" (verse 10). The death of the Messiah implies the end of the sacrifices that pointed to Him.

As a result, the covenant is broadened. Since it no longer depends upon the Temple and the sacrifices, the covenant becomes universal. History has confirmed theological truth. For both Christians and Jews the destruction of the Temple just a few years later moved the religious experience away from the sacrifices in Jerusalem to a more spiritual and universal realm.

All the events outlined in the prophecy of the final week of the 70 weeks met their fulfillment in history. Nothing in the prophetic text allows for the dispensationalist speculation that postpones the last week to the end-time. On the contrary, the data of the text, the literary structure, and the lexical and theological associations present strong evidence for the unity of the prophetic vision: the Messiah's death is associated with a universal covenant and with the end of sacrifice and offering. Even the numeric arrangement of 70 weeks suggests a continuous line. The number 7 introduces and concludes the prophetic period: 7 (weeks), 62 (weeks), 7 (days). It is also significant that the same disjunctive accent, the *athnach,* is placed on both periods of time, the first 7 (Daniel 9:24) and the last 7 (verse 27). This not only points out and emphasizes[11] the significance of the number 7, but also implies that just as the first period of "7" is not separated from the other weeks, so is it for the last period of "7." The same observation holds in regard to the relationship between the 70 years of Jeremiah's prophecy and the 70-weeks prophecy as reported in Daniel 9:2, 24-27. The echo between the two prophetic periods of 70 that frame Daniel's prayer (verses 3-23) suggests that the two prophecies concern an event of the same historical reality (both will take place in history) and of the same spiritual vein (the hope of the return from exile and the hope of the messianic redemption). This parallel between the periods of 70 also implies that just as the 70 years of the Babylonian exile are continuous, so are the 70 weeks of Daniel's prophecy.

Indeed, the entire dispensationalist scenario of a covenant between the antichrist and Israel in the "postponed" last week of human history goes against the plain and intentional meaning of the prophetic text. This fact by itself should be enough to question the validity of the dispensationalist prophetic interpretation of Israel.

### 3. THE REGATHERING OF ISRAEL

We now understand why for dispensationalists it is a proper conclusion that when Israel has returned to the land, it is in preparation for the end of the age. In fact, they consider such a return "prophetically necessary." Since the signing of a seven-year covenant between the antichrist and Israel precedes the great tribulation, "it is transparent that in order for such a covenant to be fulfilled, the children of Israel had to be in their ancient land and had to be organized into a political unit suitable for such a covenant relationship."[12] Since the Jews have now regained their ancestral land, the dispensationalists conclude that the time of the end, is at hand. They then interpret the return of the Jews to the Holy Land as a sign of the end, preparation for the establishment of the postponed earthly kingdom of Israel. Dispensationalists support their interpretation primarily on the Old Testament return prophecies of Isaiah, Jeremiah, and Ezekiel.

*The return prophecies.* "It shall come to pass in that day that the Lord shall set His hand again the second time to recover the remnant of His people who are left, from Assyria and Egypt" (Isa. 11:11), Dispensationalists stress the phrase "second time" to imply that the return from Babylon represented the "first-time" restoration, while a future return to the Holy Land would constitute a "second time." They conclude that Isaiah foresaw the present Zionist movement. Yet the concluding statement of Isaiah's prophetic text makes it clear that this return for the second time concerns those taken captive in Assyria: "There will be a highway for the remnant of His people who will be left from Assyria, as it was for Israel in the day that he came up from the land of Egypt" (verse 16). The prophet is alluding to a comparable situation for the exiles of the northern kingdom. Just as God made the way for Israel to leave Egypt, so also will He make a way for Israel to return from Assyrian exile. The mention of places that seem to be located outside the strict borders of the

Assyrian Empire is not surprising considering the extent of the Assyrian conquests. They stretched as far as Egypt (and therefore Pathros and Cush) and included the Phoenician coastland (Hamath and the islands) and Elam (old Persia) and Shinar (Babylon). Also the list follows a diagonal course from the north (Assyria) to the south (Egypt, Pathros, Cush)[13] and from the east (Elam and Shinar) to the west (Hamath and the islands),[14] thus suggesting and anticipating the "four corners of the earth" (verse 12), a stylistic way of implying the totality of the Assyrian exile.

As for the reference in verse 10 to "the Root of Jesse," who will, like a banner, attract Gentiles as well as Jews, it applies to the coming of the Messiah, who will extend the covenant and salvation not only to the Jews but also to people from many nations. It also conveys the future perspective of the eschatological cosmic peace on earth when "the wolf . . . shall dwell with the lamb" (verse 6) and there shall be no more hurt or destruction, "for the earth shall be full of the knowledge of the Lord as the waters cover the sea" (verse 9).

Later in his book the prophet Isaiah links the promise of the return from the Babylonian exile, through Cyrus, king of Persia (Isa. 44:26-28; 45:1-13; 52:8), to the messianic hope of "everlasting salvation" (Isa. 45:17).[15]

Other prophets attest to the same kind of association and linkage. Jeremiah's prophecies clearly apply historically to the return from Babylon. He explicitly refers to a return both in space (Babylon [Jer. 16:14, 15]) and in time (after 70 years [Jer. 25:12]). The prophet also associates the expectation of this specific return with messianic and even eschatological hope. Some passages link the anticipation of the return from Babylon with the hope of the "new covenant" that God will put in the heart (Jer. 31:31, 32).

It is the experience that New Testament writers apply to the first coming of the Messiah (Heb. 8:8-12; 10:16, 17; 2 Cor. 3:3). Jeremiah even uses the imagery to depict the hope of the eschatological coming of the Lord that will bring judgment, righteousness, and peace on the earth (Jer. 23:5, 6; 33:15, 16).

Likewise, Ezekiel's prophecies concern the same past historical event of the return from Babylonian-Assyrian captivity (see Eze. 1:1-3). His book also explicitly mentions the exile to Babylon and the return from it (Eze. 11:24; 16:28; 33:21, 22). It gives the moment of the return from the perspective of the Israelites of that time—as an event "about to come" (Eze. 36:8). The prophecy is clearly situated within the contemporary predicament of the Israelites in the Babylonian exile. The prophet hears them saying: "Our bones are dry, our hope is lost, and we ourselves are cut off!" (Eze. 37:11).

Also, as in Jeremiah and Isaiah, Ezekiel describes the return from Babylonian exile as a great moment of hope. The prophet used it as an opportunity to elaborate about an even more wonderful hope, the hope of the first coming of the Messiah, who would initiate the experience of the "new covenant" (Eze. 11:19, 20; 16:61-63; 36:24-30) and usher in everlasting peace and the effective presence of God (Eze. 37:24-27; 43:6, 7; 48:35).

But this constant and systematic association between the return prophecies and messianic, eschatological deliverance does not mean this gathering of Israel leads immediately to the coming of the Messiah and therefore concerns a gathering of the Jews at the end of time. It also does not mean that we should interpret them as "conditional prophecies" that have not been fulfilled, or will never be, because of Israel's unfaithfulness. As we saw, the plain and explicit sense of the passages and their contexts make it clear that such passages refer to the now-past return from the Babylonian exile. The reason for such association involves the Hebrew concept of time being bound up with its context and even identified with it. Thus in Hebrew thinking, "matters which are widely separated with reference to time can, if their content coincides, be identified and regarded as simultaneous." [16] We can observe this perspective in the Jewish feasts that link past and future events. The past events of Creation and the Exodus are associated with the Sabbath (Ex. 20:11; Deut. 5:15). Likewise, the future event of God's salvation has become identified with the sabbatical year, or the jubilee (2 Chron. 36:21; Isa. 61:1, 2; Lev. 25:9). The same principle appears in biblical prophecies, which, for instance, invoke the great battle of Jezreel (2 Kings 10:11) to speak about the future eschatological battle (Hosea 1:4, 11). The past event of Sodom serves as a vehicle to describe the similar fate of a future city (Lam. 4:6; Rev. 11:8). A good illustration of this concept appears in the New Testament in which Jesus unites His prophecy concerning the soon destruction of the Temple and Jerusalem (Matt. 24:1, 2) with far distant events of the end and the destruction of the world (verses 3-31).

*The reconstruction of the Temple.* The same reservations apply to the so-called predictions of the reconstruction of the Temple and the hope of again offering Levitical sacrifices. Dispensationalists use excavations of the wall of the Temple, research about the ark of the covenant, and, most of all, the activities of the "Institute of the Temple" at Jerusalem as arguments to support their thesis that one day the Temple will be rebuilt and God will allow sacrifices to be forever offered on the altar. But such an interpretation contradicts the New Testament teaching that animal sacrifices are no longer relevant in view of the ultimate sacrifice of Christ (Heb. 10:1-4). Jewish tradition also explains the sacrifices as a *"halakha* ["a traditional law"] regarding the Messiah."[17] In fact, the restoration of sacrifices would contradict the very essence of rabbinic Judaism that emphasizes the superiority of prayers over sacrifices[18] and affirms, on the basis of biblical references (Ps. 141:2; Hosea 14:2), that, after the destruction of the Temple in A.D. 70, prayers have been substituted for sacrifices.[19] This principle has in fact inspired the whole structure of post-Temple Jewish liturgy. The *Shacharit* prayer has replaced the morning *tamid* and the *Minchah* prayer the afternoon *tamid*. When an additional sacrifice was necessary, the rabbis introduced the *Musaf* prayer.[20]

Therefore, the wish to see sacrifices offered again on the altar ignores the Jewish views on that matter. In fact, most Jews and Israelis reject the whole notion. Reform and Conservative Jews, who represent a large majority of Judaism, have entirely abolished any liturgical references to sacrifice. Even the Orthodox minority that still entertains the hope of this restoration insists that "the revival of the sacrificial service must . . . be sanctioned by the divine voice of a prophet. The mere acquisition of the Temple Mount or of all Palestine by Jews, by war, or political combination, would not justify the revival."[21] And even the perspective of "the divine voice of a prophet" is problematic, since the dominant view in traditional Judaism is that prophecy came to an end in biblical times and the Shekinah departed from Israel.[22] As for the sporadic attempts of groups such as the Temple Mount Faithful, who seem to promote the idea of the reconstruction of the Temple with the possible restoration of sacrifices, they receive no support from Israeli authorities and are far from being representative of the general trend of traditional Judaism. The Israeli press regularly characterizes them by such epithets as "a bunch of nuts" or "dangerous lunatics."[23] In fact, any prophetic claim on that matter, whether it comes from Jews, Palestinians, or Christians, is an extremely dangerous argument. History has shown that such thinking has always led to fanaticism or insanity and inspired the worst crimes. Furthermore, to imply the supernatural leaves no room for any negotiation, because who can debate with God?

*Dispensationalism and anti-Semitism.* The truth is that most Israelis and informed Jews regard this "Christian" obsession with prophecies to justify the success of Israel or any future Jewish endeavor as suspect. Behind such seemingly enthusiastic support of Israel lurks the ghost of anti-Semitism. The way it perceives the Jew as "peculiarly different because God made him different"[24] betrays the old prejudice and contains the potential for dangerous racist speculation with all the traditional anti-Semitic myths and stereotypes. "Why are the Jews so maligned and hated when they are so productive and helpful?" television evangelist Jack Van Impe asked in *Israel's Final Holocaust:* "There can be but one explanation—the fulfillment of prophecy." On the basis of certain Deuteronomic passages, Van Impe concludes: "In short, although the material gains brought by Jews are desired, the Jew himself is unwanted. . . . Their skill in handling money has often brought them grief."[25] Paul Boyer describes the dispensationalist view of the Jews as a "complex system: . . . a theological mask for Jew hatred." For although "it incorporates many philosemitic elements . . . important structural components of this ideology encourage an obsessive preoccupation with the Jews as a people eternally set apart, about whom sweeping generalizations can be made with the sanction of biblical authority."[26]

The scenario imagined by dispensationalists confirms such a suspicion. The prophetic fulfillment that seems to benefit the Jews actually hides a baleful plan that aims at crushing them. For dispensationalists the return of the Jews to Palestine should lead to an unprecedented wave of anti-Semitism, justified on account of the collective guilt of Israel for Jesus' death. "Of course, all the world is guilty of piercing the Son of God," writes one dispensationalist theologian, "but the Jews were particular instruments in that respect."[27] And for that reason, observes another, anti-Semitism will "grow worse and worse" until the tribulation, when "the nations will gather to deliver the remnant of Israel the coup de grâce."[28] Although Hal Lindsey deplores the "insane flames" of Jew hatred, he refers to the Scriptures to justify anti-Semitism that will reach "its most feverish pitch at the time of the end."[29] Van Impe describes this "final Holocaust" both as an expression of God's will and as motivated by Satan.[30] For dispensationalism the most tragic chapter of Jewish history still lies ahead. Cursed by God, the Jews will suffer as long as human history continues, until the coming of Christ, when Jews will finally recognize Him as their Messiah and will then all be saved.

## 4. THE SALVATION OF ISRAEL

The dispensational position is that all living Jews who have regathered in Palestine will ultimately be saved by seeing the return of Christ. As one prominent dispensationalist author states: "The whole of Jacob's bodily descendants then living on earth shall attain to faith through sight of the returning Messiah."[31]

First of all, we must recognize that this concept of salvation through sight contradicts the general teaching of Scripture, which presents salvation through faith (Rom. 4:3) and questions the validity of a faith based on visible manifestations (John 20:29; Matt. 12:38, 39). Furthermore, no biblical prophecy supports such an idea.

The thesis that "all" the Jews will be saved cannot be defended exegetically on the basis of Paul's statement in Romans 11:26: "All Israel will be saved." Indeed, a close examination of the context of this key proof text reveals that the conclusion of Paul's dissertation about Israel actually points in another direction.

Paul has just explained to the converted Gentiles, who bragged about their spiritual superiority over the unbelieving Jews, that their behavior was inappropriate: "Do not boast against the branches" (verse 18). In order to make his point, the apostle relates the salvation of the Gentiles to the salvation of the Jews. If it became possible for the Gentiles to be grafted to the tree and become partakers "of the root and fatness of the olive tree" (verse 17), it is precisely because some branches of the natural tree were broken off (verse 19). Paul repeats his reasoning, reminding the reader of what he calls "this mystery," namely, that the "partial hardening has happened to Israel until the fullness of the Gentiles has come in" (verse 25, NASB).

If, on the other hand, it was possible for Gentiles to be "grafted contrary to nature into a cultivated olive tree, how much more will these, who are natural branches, be grafted into their own olive tree" (verse 24). It must be pointed out that Paul is not suggesting the salvation of all the Jews, just as he does not imply the salvation of all the Gentiles. In both cases, only "some" are concerned; only some wild branches, Gentiles, will be "grafted in among" some of the natural "branches [Jews] which were broken off" (verse 17). Likewise, only "some" natural branches will be regrafted. Significantly Paul designates the regrafted Jews with the word "these," thus referring back to "some of the branches" that have been broken off (verses 17, 19, 22). Paul is consistent on this restriction throughout his reasoning, since in verse 25 he qualifies this "hardening," which affects Israel as only "partial."

It is these "two" salvations implied in Paul's conclusion: "And so all Israel will be saved" (verse 26). The phrase "all Israel" is a technical expression that has an eschatological connotation (see above). The "Israel" in view here is the saved people, Jews and Gentiles, who will inherit the heavenly kingdom.

We see this interpretation further confirmed in verse 32, which again uses the same word "all": "For God has committed them *all* to disobedience, that He might have mercy on *all.*" The context of this verse is the same as that in verse 26, and the argument is also the same, namely, the connection between the salvation of the Gentiles and that of the Jews.

Paul starts in verses 26 and 27 with the salvation of the Jews, included in "all Israel," thus continuing the line of argument of verse 24 that deals with the salvation of the Jews. Then in verses 28-30 he turns to the Gentiles and argues again that they are saved thanks to the unfaithfulness of some Jews: "Concerning the gospel they are enemies for your sake" (verse 28). . . . "You . . . have now obtained mercy through their disobedience" (verse 30). In verse 31 he shifts to the concern about the Jews and argues in a reverse manner that the salvation of the disobedient Jews is also related to the salvation of the disobedient Gentiles: "Through the mercy shown you [Gentiles] they [Jews] also may obtain mercy."

In conclusion Paul infers a theological lesson about the salvation of both groups of people: "God has committed them all to disobedience, that He might have mercy on all" (verse 32). He has described both peoples as disobedient, the Gentiles in verse 30 and the Jews in verse 31. The "all" whom God "committed . . . to disobedience" applies therefore to both the Jews and the Gentiles, just as with the "all" for whom He had mercy.

The parallelism of reasoning, along with the common wording and context between the two verses (verses 26, 32), suggest that the "all" in verse 32 conveys the same meaning as the "all" in verse 26. The "all Israel" who will be saved (verse 26) implies both Gentiles and Jews.

From the perspective of salvation, Paul concludes, Gentiles have now joined Jews in becoming Israel. The concept is not new. It was a common experience in the historical Israel of the Old Testament (see below), and it was the hope of the prophets of Israel. One of them, Isaiah, refers explicitly to "the sons of the foreigner who join themselves to the Lord, to serve Him" (Isa. 56:6). He describes them as keeping the Sabbath and holding fast the same covenant (verse 4). The following verses clearly outline the prophetic ideal:

" 'For My house shall be called a house of prayer for all nations.' The Lord God, who gathers the outcasts of Israel, says, 'Yet I will gather to him others besides those who are gathered to him' " (Isa 56:7, 8).

It is a picture that completely contradicts the theological eternal apartheid of the dispensationalist worldview.

---

[1] For the history of the dispensationlist idea, see Arnold D. Ehlert, comp., *A Bibliographic History of Dispensationalism* (Grand Rapids: Baker Book House, 1965).

[2] See Jacques Doukhan, *Hebrew for Theologians: A Textbook for the Study of Biblical Hebrew in Relation to Hebrew Thinking* (Lanham, Md.: University Press of America, Inc., 1993), pp. 192, 193.

[3] See Sanhedrin 56a; Hullin 92a.

[4] See especially David Flusser, "The Jewish-Christian Schism, Part II," *Immanuel* 17 (Winter 1983/1984): 32-38.

[5] This phrase belongs to both thematic lines (A and B), since it concerns both the time of the future coming of the Messiah and the future fate of Jerusalem. Yet it does not contain any of the specific keywords *(shavu' or chrts)* normally associated respectively to those two themes (Messiah, Jerusalem). We therefore put this phrase outside of the thematic lines as an autonomous feature on which depends the development of both lines.

[6] This more appropriate translation takes into consideration the participle form of the verb (a translation is suggested in a note in the NKJV).

[7] See Ex. 24:8; 34:27; Joshua 9:15; Hosea 2:18; Jer. 34:13; etc.

[8] Joyce G. Baldwin, *Daniel: An Introduction and Commentary,* Tyndale Old Testament Commentaries (Downers Grove, Ill.: InterVarsity Press, 1978), p. 171.

[9] Stephen R. Miller, *Daniel,* The New American Commentary (Nashville: Broadman & Holman Publishers, 1994), p. 271.

[10] See Doukhan, "Seventy Weeks," pp. 20, 21.

[11] On the emphasis function of the *athnach,* see William Wickes, *Two Treatises on the Accentuation of the Old Testament* (New York: Ktav Publishing House, 1970), Part I, pp. 32-35; Part II, p. 4; see also Jacques Doukhan, *Secrets of Daniel* (Hagerstown, Md.: Review and Herald Pub. Assn., 2000), pp. 146, 147.

[12] John F. Walvoord, *The Church in Prophecy* (Grand Rapids: Zondervan Pub. House, 1964), p. 173.

[13] Pathros is associated with Egypt (see Eze. 29:14; Jer. 44:1, 15); Cush—that is, Ethiopia or Nubia—was always associated with Egypt, either as a subjugated or a dominating power.

[14] The Hebrew word for "islands," *'im,* refers to the Phoenician coast rather than to the islands of the Mediterranean Sea (see Eze. 26:15).

[15] Likewise, Isaiah places the coming of the "Suffering Servant," who will atone for our sin (Isa. 53), in the perspective of the eschatological and universal salvation (Isa. 56:6-8; 65:17-25; 66:22-24).

[16] E. Jenni, "Time," in *The Interpreter's Dictionary of the Bible,* vol. 4, p. 646.

[17] Zebahim 44a; Sanhedrin 51b.

[18] See Berakoth 32b.

[19] See Yoma 86b; Megillah 31b; Ta'anith 27b.

[20] Berakoth 4:1, 7; 26b.

[21] Michael Friedländer, *The Jewish Religion* (New York: Pardes Pub. House, 1946), p. 417.

[22] Yoma 9b.

[23] See, for instance, "Assault on the Mount," Jerusalem *Post*, Nov. 3, 1989, p. 12.

[24] Frederic J. Miles, *Prophecy, Past, Present and Prospective* (Grand Rapids: Zondervan Pub. House, 1943), p. 30.

[25] Jack Van Impe and Roger F. Campbell, *Israel's Final Holocaust* (Troy, Mich.: Jack Van Impe Ministries, 1979), pp. 77, 78, 81.

[26] Paul Boyer, *When Time Shall Be No More: Prophecy Belief in Modern American Culture* (Cambridge, Mass.: Belknap Press of Harvard University Press, 1992), p. 224.

[27] Ray C. Stedman, *What's This World Coming To? An Expository Study of Matthew 24-25, the Olivet Discourse,* 2nd ed. (Ventura, Calif.: Regal Books, 1986), p. 101.

[28] Louis S. Bauman, "Many Antichrists," in *Israel's Restoration: A Series of Lectures by Bible Expositors Interested in the Evangelization of the Jews,* ed. John W. Bradbury (New York: Iversen-Ford Associates, 1959), p. 69.

[29] Hal Lindsey, *There's a New World Coming: "A Prophetic Odyssey"* (New York: Bantam Books, 1984), p. 170.

[30] Van Impe and Campbell, pp. 27, 145.

[31] Erich Sauer, *From Eternity to Eternity: An Outline of the Divine Purposes,* trans. G. H. Lang (Grand Rapids: William B. Eerdmans, 1954), pp. 159, 160.

# The Two-Witnesses Theory

Against the rejection-supersessionist theory, which excludes Israel and the law from the plan of salvation, and the dispensationalist theory, which dissociates the church, grace, and Jesus from Israel and the law, I would like to suggest a third option that will favor the idea of complementarity between the two peoples and the revelations they represent. In this view, both peoples, the church and Israel, were needed as God's people, but not in the sense that God contracted two different and parallel covenants (i.e., dispensationalism). And also not in the sense that God contracted two successive covenants: the second (the "new") replacing the first (the "old" [i.e., rejection-supersessionist theory]). For God's initial plan was, indeed, to have only "one people" to witness to Him.

But an accident of history occurred, "the mystery of lawlessness" (2 Thess. 2:7), as Paul described it, that kept the Jews from accepting Jesus in a dramatic manner. It thereby produced by necessity two separate entities, Israel and the church, each one claiming the right of being God's people. But in fact, each was witnessing to a truth that was missing in the other. Israel had the law but without Jesus, and the church had Jesus but increasingly downplayed the law, thus making their separate presence on the scene of salvation history necessary.

This scenario seems to be the one sketched by the apocalyptic passage of Revelation 11:3 that speaks of two witnesses who would receive the mission to "prophesy," that is, to testify of the revelation from above. It is interesting to note that it associates the two witnesses through the miracles they perform with two key figures from the Hebrew Scriptures, namely, Moses and Elijah. The turning of water into blood and the plagues allude to Moses (Rev. 11:6; cf. Ex. 7:14-18). The fire that devours the enemy and the rain that is blocked point to Elijah (Rev. 11:5, 6; cf. 1 Kings 19:10; 17:1). The only text in the Old Testament coupling the two figures appears in Malachi, the last prophet of the Hebrew Scriptures: "Remember the law of my servant Moses, the decrees and laws I gave him at Horeb for all Israel. See, I will send you the prophet Elijah before that great and dreadful day of the Lord comes" (Mal. 4:4, 5, NIV).

The passage has a dual orientation. First, it refers us back to Moses—the past. It is a call to "remember" and to remain faithful to the old covenant. Hence, Moses represents the Old Testament. Christians during the time of John associated Moses with the Torah and the revelation of the Old Testament (e.g., Matt. 23:2; John 1:17; Acts 15:21). According to Jewish tradition, the Torah originated with Moses: "Moses received the Torah at Sinai and transmitted it to Joshua. Joshua transmitted it to the elders, and the elders to the prophets, and the prophets to the members of the Assembly."[1]

The second orientation, which refers to Elijah, looks to the future. It is the promise of the coming of the Messiah and the kindling of hope. Christians during the time of John linked the arrival of the Messiah with the prophet Elijah (Luke 1:13-17; Matt. 17:10-13). Likewise, Jewish tradition relates the person of Elijah to the messianic hope in much the same way. In it Elijah is not only a precursor, but an active agent, of the Messiah.[2] Legends, liturgical gestures on the eve of Passover (the Seder), and songs on the Shabbat all call upon Elijah in expectation of the Messiah. Thus Moses refers us back to the Torah, the Old Testament; while Elijah propels us forward in the messianic hope of the New Testament.

Considering the Judeo-Christian background of John, this allusion to Moses and Elijah is no coincidence. It is strongly evocative of the two revelations of God received by the early Christians, namely, the so-called Old Testament and the New Testament.[3] Both witnesses are present and play a part in the prophetic process. This dual reference brings out the relevance of the entire Bible, emphasizing the complementarity of and the need for the two testimonies.

But beyond the allusion to the two inspired documents, we also have the reference to the two peoples who have "transmitted" them. Indeed, the prophet's main concern lies with the men and women who prophesy and who suffer (Rev. 11:3, 7). The two witnesses could then be historical and traditional Israel (for the Old Testament) and the historical and traditional church (for the New Testament). By "witnesses," I do not mean an "ideal" holy community (i.e, the "remnant" or the "redeemed"), but simply a people whose existence and history bear testimony to the historical fact of revelation. In that sense, in spite of their respective deficiencies Israel and the church are in history the visible and tangible witnesses to God's revelation. And even if we disagree with this apocalyptic interpretation or this biblical reference, it remains a historical and undeniable fact that we owe the Holy Scriptures, God's written revelation, to the faithful work of transmission and incarnated testimony of both Israel and the church. This historical fact alone should be enough to justify the metaphoric use of the concept of "the two witnesses," the Old Testament legal requirement to establish the truth (Num. 35:30) and a practice recognized by Jesus Himself: "The testimony of two men is true" (John 8:17).

## 1. ISRAEL AND THE CHURCH[4]

We do not need to allude to the fact that early Christianity was Jewish. Not only the Messiah but also His disciples, initial followers, and the first missionaries were Jewish. Christianity arose from within Israel. In addition, we should also remember that according to the testimony of the Gospels, the majority of the Jewish population (from the beginning to the end of Jesus' ministry) gladly received the Christian message. Furthermore, recent scholarship[5] has demonstrated that, contrary to popular thought, the Christian mission to the Jews was highly successful in the beginning. On the basis of the records of the book of Acts (Acts 4:4; 5:14; 6:7; 9:35; 21:20), sociological and statistical analysis, archaeological evidence, and the testimony of Ethiopian tradition, it has been established that many Jews—and in some places almost all of them—accepted Jesus as their Messiah. We now have reason to believe that in spite of some tensions, the majority of the Jewish population reached by the early Jewish Christians were convinced by their testimony. It may even be suggested that the trend was such that one might fear that the whole people of Israel were in the process of accepting Christ. While this may sound exaggerated, let's not forget that this prospect was already looming in the time of Jesus, according to Caiaphas's prophetic intuition (John 11:50).

The difficulty we have is that we tend to read past history from the point of view of present reality. The majority of Jews today do not have Jesus, and that has been the case for centuries. It is, therefore, difficult for us to imagine a time when things were different. In fact, it was only later that the trend reversed and Jews ceased to be open to the Christian message. The question naturally arises: If so many Jews accepted Jesus in the early days of the church, what changed the direction of history? The fact that "Jews continued as a significant source of Christian converts until . . . as late as the fourth century,"[6] a period historically associated with the formal rejection of the law of God[7] and more particularly of the Sabbath, suggests that the Jewish resistance to the Christian message was essentially because of the Christian rejection of the law. As Jewish historian Jules Isaac puts it: "The Jewish rejection of Christ was triggered by the Christian rejection of the Law."[8] Or in the words of church historian Marcel Simon: "The rejection of Israel [by the church] is the inevitable corollary of the abrogation of the law."[9]

Focusing on the issue of the Sabbath, Christian theologian Marvin Wilson observes: "This move to Sunday worship made it exceedingly difficult, if not virtually impossible, for a Jew to give any serious consideration to the Christian message. . . . In short, to become a Christian was considered as leaving behind the Jewishness of one's past, hardly a live option for any faithful Jew to consider."[10] For Jewish theologian David Novak, it is this diminution of "the binding norms of the Torah" that the rabbis offered "as the prime reason for their rejection of . . . Christianity . . . as an acceptable form of Judaism itself."[11]

Indeed, contrary to what many people, both Jews and Christians, think, it was on the law, the very place of Jewish identity, that Jews and Christians departed from each other. As Professor James D. G. Dunn notes: "Insofar as Judaism regarded the law . . . as integral to its identity, and continued to do so in a rabbinic Judaism which organized itself round the Torah, . . . a parting of the ways [was] inevitable."[12] It was on the law and not on the messianic controversy that the Jewish-Christian separation took place. Significantly, James Parkes notices "a strange and tragic fact" that Judeo-Christians were excommunicated by Gentile Christians, "not for inadequate Christology but because they still observed 'the Law.'"[13] It was not the Messiah—the issue of Jesus—that caused problems for the Jew, but the abrogation of the law that went with it. Indeed, Jewish tradition and history attest to a great number of messianic views and experiences that blurred and even crossed the borders between Judaism and Christianity, messianic views that are at times bolder than the Christian counterpart.[14]

## 2. TORAH AND MESSIAH

The schism between what some have called "the mother and daughter religions"[15] did not only separate and oppose two groups designed to be one within Israel (or the church); it also affected the testimony of the revealed truth.

From the time of the division onward, Israel was no longer able to hear the Christian testimony about Jesus, because it had become associated with the rejection of the law. Likewise, the church has been deaf to the Jewish testimony of the Torah, because it has associated it with the rejection of Jesus. This is a tragedy. But at the same time, the survival of these two distinct groups, each one witnessing to the truth absent in the other, makes it clear that they need each other to come to the "gospel in its fullness." The Christian rejection of the Torah calls for the testimony of Israel. Ironically, Christians have traditionally recognized this providential role and mission of the Jews as guardians of the law. For example, in the Middle Ages Pope Innocent III (1198-1217) argued that the Jews "ought not to be slain, lest the Christian people forget divine Law."[16] Likewise, the Jewish ignorance of the Messiah requires the testimony of the church. In other words, the deficiency in the testimony of the one has made necessary the preservation of the testimony of the other, a type of reasoning reflected in Paul's parable of the olive tree. The cutting of the natural branches allows for the grafting of the wild branches: "Now if their fall is riches for the world, and their failure riches for the Gentiles, how much more their fullness!" (Rom. 11:12). Whatever interpretation we may give to that passage, it suggests from the outset some kind of dependence between the two communities of faith. The stumbling of Israel was salvation for the Gentile Christians, and, on the other hand, the salvation of the Gentiles was supposed to provoke the jealousy of Israel for their own salvation. In a similar way, we may observe the same type of relationship between the two groups in regard to the testimony that concerns the Torah and the Messiah. It is the fall of the church in regard to the Torah that has preserved the calling of Israel. Also, it is the ignorance of Israel regarding Jesus that has safeguarded the calling of the church. Interestingly, a resolution passed some 20 years ago by the Synod of the Protestant Church of the Rhineland came to the same conclusion: "We believe that in their calling Jews and Christians are always witnesses of God in the presence of the world and before each other."[17]

The historical presence of both witnesses does not mean there are two ways of salvation (or two covenants). There is only one, the salvation provided by God Himself through His incarnation and sacrifice (John 14:6). But this salvation does not exclude faithfulness to the law. On the contrary, it implies it all the more (Rom. 6:1, 2). This is God's message to humanity—to the church and Israel—as He allowed the two witnesses to survive.

The present situation and the actual course of history were also not in God's plan. The existing dichotomy between Torah and Messiah (dispensationalism) was not God's will. Nor was the integration of Israel into an "apostate" church (rejection-supersessionism) His desire. Rather, we should regard this separation as a tragic wound because of the failure on both sides.

Paul's imagery of the olive tree in Romans 11 suggests that God's plan was that Israel should have blossomed in the church through Jesus, and that the church should have enrooted itself in Israel through the revealed law. That is why the dispensationalist proposal is not satisfactory. Instead of recognizing the separation as a product of iniquity, it justifies and interprets it as an eternal fact that was the doing of God Himself.

The rejection-supersessionist theory is not to be retained either, for it implies that the church, which has defined itself through rejection of its Jewish roots, has replaced Israel, thus resulting in apostasy and failure. The church has manifested its apostasy through its abandonment of God's revealed law. And it has demonstrated its failure through a history of oppression and anti-Semitism climaxing in the Holocaust.

That is why what Paul calls "the stumbling of some Jews," which took place while the church was still within Israel and had not yet rejected its Jewish roots and the law, is of a different nature than the accusation of rejection would be at another time and set of circumstances. After the apostasy of the church, with its pagan course and oppressive behavior, the issue of the Jewish rejection of the Christian message has taken another dimension and meaning. For, if in the time of Jesus, Paul, or even John, it was still possible for a Jew to accept Christ, after the Jewish-Christian separation (and all that followed) it became almost impossible. Jewish theologian David Blumenthal states: "Finally, the bloody history of Christian-Jewish relations over two millennia does not allow the traditional Jew to identify with a doctrine that is specifically Christian, even if it were otherwise true. Christianity has simply been too cruel to Jews and Judaism, even if, in very recent times, some Christians have taken a different attitude toward us."[18]

What was allowed to be said and thought in early Christianity about a Jewish stumbling is no longer possible and permissible after the tragedy of the Jewish-Christian separation. Even if Paul in his context had the reason and right to speak of the stumbling of some Jews who rejected the gospel at that time, in our contemporary context we do not have the same right or reasons. What's more, if Paul in his time refused to endorse the rejection-supersessionist theory, after the apostasy of the church, 2,000 years of anti-Semitism, and the Holocaust it has become all the more absurd to speak of the rejection of Israel and of its replacement by the church. It has even become somewhat humorous to suggest, along the lines of Paul's reasoning, that the Jews would be made jealous by the testimony of the Christians.

Now, even if for some reason there should still remain any doubt in our minds about this line of interpretation, the arguments for rejection and nonrejection, as far as they appear to be of *equal weight,* should be decided by the argument of love and ethics. For it is preferable to choose the interpretation that leads to love rather than the one that results in hatred and contempt. The fruit of love and the guidance of ethics should serve as the ultimate test to evaluate and control our reading of the Bible. Otherwise, we will be in great danger of reading the Bible, once again, in a way that will lead–in fact, *has led*—to the Holocaust.[19] In addition to careful exegetical analysis of the several texts, we need to take seriously the lessons of history.

From a Seventh-day Adventist perspective, the rejection-supersessionist theory is even more problematic, because Seventh-day Adventist theology clearly identifies the rejection of the law by the church as a sign of apostasy. Thus, for Ellen G. White the Christian abandonment of the law is a sin of the same gravity as the Jewish spurning of Jesus: "When the Jews rejected Christ they rejected the foundation of their faith. And, on the other hand, the Christian world of today who claim faith in Christ, but reject the law of God, are making a mistake similar to that of the deceived Jews."[20] Furthermore, Ellen White's parallel between "the Jews" and "the Christian world" suggests that since she could not have implied all the Christian world (for many Christians keep the law), likewise she did not imply all the Jews. We must therefore understand her reference to the two entities in a limited and generic sense.

The question should arise, then, for those Adventists who still hold the supersessionist view: If the church has replaced Israel, then which church? And if we answer, "the church consisting of the early Christians in Paul's time," we should then realize that at that time the church did not yet exist as a separate entity. Christianity was still a Jewish phenomenon taking place in the spiritual confines of Israel. Or if we refer to an invisible "remnant," we should also recognize that this is not a replacement, since there has always existed a remnant. This invisible "new" remnant is at most a continuation of the old. But whatever answer we may give to that question, we are still embarrassed because of the long span of time between those early Christians and the Adventist Church.

---

[1] Pirkey Aboth 1.1.

[2] See Sanhedrin 98a; Pesikta Rabbati 35.16; Leviticus Rabbah 34.8; etc.

[3] See Ellen White: "The two witnesses represent the Scriptures of the Old and the New Testament" (*The Great Controversy,* p. 267).

[4] For more discussion on this topic, see J. Doukhan, *Israel and the Church.*

[5] See especially Rodney Stark, *The Rise of Christianity: A Sociologist Reconsiders History* (Princeton, N.J.: Princeton University Press, 1996). Cf. Jacob Jervell, *Luke and the People of God: A New Look at Luke-Acts* (Minneapolis: Augsburg Pub. House, 1972), pp. 52, 53; David W. Pao, *Acts and the Isaianic New Exodus* (Tübingen: Mohr Siebeck, 2000), p. 244.

[6] Stark, p. 49.

[7] It is interesting that Ellen White associates the coming of "the mystery of iniquity" and "the development of the 'man of sin'" with the conversion of Constantine in the fourth century. At that time, she says, "persecution ceased, and Christianity entered the courts and palaces . . . ; and in place of the requirements of God, she substituted human theories and traditions. . . . and the world, cloaked with a form of righteousness, walked into the church" (*The Great Controversy,* pp. 49, 50).

[8] J. Isaac, *Genèse de l'Antisémitisme,* p. 147.

[9] Marcel Simon, *Verus Israel: A Study of the Relations Between Christians and Jews in the Roman Empire, 135-425,* trans. H. McKeating (Oxford University Press, 1986), p. 169.

[10] Marvin R. Wilson, *Our Father Abraham: Jewish Roots of the Christian Faith* (Grand Rapids: William B. Eerdmans, 1989), p. 80.

[11] David Novak, *"Mitsvah,"* in *Christianity in Jewish Terms,* ed. Tikva Frymer-Kensky et al. (Boulder, Colo.: Westview Press, 2000), p. 121.

[12] James D. G. Dunn, *The Partings of the Ways Between Christianity and Judaism and Their Significance for the Character of Christianity* (London: SCM Press, 1991), p. 139.

[13] James Parkes, *The Foundations of Judaism and Christianity* (Chicago: Quadrangle Books, 1960), p. 222.

[14] See Raphael Patai, *The Messiah Texts* (New York: Avon, 1979); Dan

Cohn-Sherbok, *The Jewish Messiah* (Edinburgh: T. & T. Clark, 1979).

[15] Naomi W. Cohen, ed., *Essential Papers on Jewish-Christian Relations in the United States: Imagery and Reality* (New York: New York University Press, 1990), p. 2; Abraham Heschel, "No Religion Is an Island," *Union Seminary Quarterly Review* 21, no. 2, part 1 (1966): 124, 125.

[16] See Martin A. Cohen and Helga Croner, eds., *Christian Mission-Jewish Mission* (New York: Paulist Press, 1982), p. 26.

[17] World Council of Churches, Geneva, *Current Dialogue,* Winter 1980/1981, p. 1.

[18] David R. Blumenthal, "Tselem: Toward an Anthropopathic Theology of Image," in *Christianity in Jewish Terms,* p. 347.

[19] On this matter, see Jacques Doukhan, "Reading the Bible After Auschwitz," in *Remembering for the Future: The Holocaust in an Age of Genocide,* ed. John K. Roth and Elisabeth Maxwell, vol. 2, *Ethics and Religion* (Houndmills, Basingstoke, Hampshire, Eng.: PALGRAVE, 2001), pp. 683-699.

[20] Ellen G. White, *Selected Messages* (Washington, D.C.: Review and Herald Pub. Assn., 1958), book 1, p. 229.

# The Prophetic Role of Elijah

From a Seventh-day Adventist perspective the separation between the Torah and Jesus that triggered and accompanied the tragic rupture between Israel and the church has a particular significance. It is indeed remarkable that the Seventh-day Adventist Church is the only religious movement that ultimately brought the Messiah and the Torah together. For the first time in history, after 2,000 years of separation, the Torah and the Messiah go hand in hand. In fact, this association constitutes the backbone of Seventh-day Adventist theological identity. Interestingly, it carries the same type of tension as that involving the three angels' messages[1] about judgment and Creation. It is a tension that will ultimately associate the two truths together, the law of God and the faith of the Messiah, thus balancing faithfulness and memory of the past with anticipation of the future: "Here is the patience of the saints; here are those who keep the commandments of God and the faith of Jesus" (Rev. 14:12). This Adventist testimony did not start in a void. Indeed, we should not ignore the work of the Holy Spirit in that process. Yet it is also clear that the discovery of the two truths—"Torah and Messiah"—is historically and existentially indebted to the double testimony of the church and Israel. Without the historical testimony of the traditional church, the Seventh-day Adventist Church would not have been able to receive the truth of Jesus and the New Testament, including apocalyptic revelation. And without the testimony of Israel, Adventist Christians would not have been able to find their way to the law, the Sabbath, the dietary laws, and the Hebrew Scriptures.[2]

That is why the Seventh-day Adventist Church should not go along with dispensationalism, which separates the two economies, or with rejection-supersessionism, which uproots the one, the "new," from the other, the "old." The Seventh-day Adventist Church should rather play the prophetic role assigned to it as the Elijah, the eschatological messenger of the last moments of human history who "will turn the hearts of the fathers to the children, and the hearts of the children to their fathers" (Mal. 4:6). This last prophecy of the final canonical Old Testament prophet contains more than an allusion to a family problem, whether in the time of Malachi or at some other period. I believe it characterizes the twofold mission of the messenger of the last days, the eschatological Elijah.[3] On the one hand, this Elijah will call the church to "remember the law of Moses" (Mal. 4:4) and to prepare for "the coming of the Lord" (verse 5), a mission already suggested in the very name "Seventh-day Adventist."[4] On the other, because of this theological association bringing together the law of Moses and the hope for the coming of the Messiah, this "Elijah" will be able to promote reconciliation between the two peoples who personify these two truths. These are the two witnesses who have been so far separated, Israel and the church. In that sense the mission represented by the eschatological Elijah confirms and transcends the respective mission of Israel and the church. God summons this last witness to become the ultimate and "complete" witness, *receiving and yet not replacing* the two witnesses, who will eventually merge, not only complementing each other but also orienting and controlling each other in tension. Elijah's mission will be to proclaim the truth of the law to the church, the truth of Jesus the Messiah to Israel, and ultimately the truths of the law and Jesus to the entire world.

## 1. RECONCILIATION WITH THE JEWS

Even if we do not share the above reading of Malachi 4:6 about the fathers and the children, the objective fact that the Seventh-day Adventist Church has been able to reconcile two truths historically and existentially represented as separate and in conflict suggests this role. Therefore, the imperative and primary vocation of the Seventh-day Adventist Church should be to work toward reconciliation between the church and Israel.

By "reconciliation" I do not mean ecumenical smiles and good and empty words of peace. Nor do I advocate compromise, syncretism, and/or political maneuvers just for the sake of bringing peoples or cultures together. The work of reconciliation intended here is to be understood in the sense of what Paul calls the "ministry of reconciliation" (2 Cor. 5:19). It obliges the "ambassadors for Christ" (verse 20) to testify to the truth of the gospel, namely, "the reconciliation with God." The work of reconciliation that falls to the Seventh-day Adventist Church is, therefore, of a religious nature—an inherent part of its theology. Such reconciliation is not of a political nature. It is not the result of a mere horizontal process of ecumenical dialogue; rather, it pertains essentially to revelation. Seventh-day Adventist theology has already reconciled Torah and Messiah, receiving both as a revelation from above. For the Seventh-day Adventist Church the task of Jewish-Christian reconciliation derives from revelation and implies, therefore, a religious duty. More so, it is a part of the prophetic charge the Adventist Church has received from God.

I doubt that Adventists have yet realized that particular aspect of their prophetic role. In fact, I am not sure if they are ready to hear it and welcome it, for this role of reconciliation involves an entire program that I would like to delineate briefly.

First of all, it means work on a spiritual and theological level. It is not enough to proclaim that we *have* the doctrinal truth of reconciliation because we *have* the Torah and the Messiah. We should also *do* the reconciliation and make it alive in our life and in our historical identity. The rigor and beauty of Torah, the work of ethics in our daily life, is not incompatible with the grace and the truth of Jesus Christ. Justice (not legalism) and love (not sentimentalism) are both necessary. The Old Testament is as vital as the New. Hebrew is as important as Greek. Serious study of Scripture is as critical as mission. Concrete and physical creation and the sensory enjoyment of life are as crucial as spiritual sanctification and eschatology. We must discover that the great God in heaven is as important as the close loving Father and the sweet Jesus. The duty to remember past revelation is as fundamental as waiting for future salvation.

Seventh-day Adventism has not yet totally assumed this theological reconciliation and the difficult tension that is the essence of its identity. We tend to ignore or emphasize one at the expense of the other. Generally, it is the Jewish side—the Torah—that gets neglected in good conscience on behalf of the other side, the "Christian." Indeed, the ordinary Adventist feels more comfortable being identified as "Christian" (i.e., they live in a Christian society and come from traditional Christian families). More important, they sometimes personally do not like to be thought of as Jews or even to be suspected of Judaizing. It is as if they have forgotten history, the very history they have been called to repair. Such fear—this anti-Semitic repulsion—took the Christians out of their natural roots in the first place and led them to apostasy.

For that reason we also need to work on another reconciliation that addresses this very phobia. I am referring to reconciliation with the Jews, not just in theory within one's own sanitized theology, but in reality with the person in flesh and in history. It means to repair the emotional and historical breach of two millennia of anti-Semitism and heal the wound that still bleeds. The temptation is to avoid the problem and refuse to face reality—to claim that "we have no sin"; that "anti-Semitism does not exist in our church." The apostle John warns against this self-righteous and deceitful mentality: "If we say we have no sin, we deceive ourselves, and the truth is not in us" (1 John 1:8; cf. Jer. 2:35; Prov. 28:13). The fundamental prerequisite for addressing the problem of anti-Semitism is to have the courage, the honesty, and the humility to recognize that the iniquity of anti-Semitism could exist in our community, church, words, and even in our minds. We should learn to be sensitive and perceptive enough to identify anti-Semitism when it manifests itself.

## 2. THE FACE OF ANTI-SEMITISM

The German agitator Wilhelm Marr coined the term *anti-*

*Semitism* in 1879 to designate current anti-Jewish campaigns in Europe. Although Arabs and others are also Semites, the word soon encompassed all forms of hostility, contempt, or bias specifically directed toward Jews.

We will present a brief overview of the history, and a description of the religious and psychological characteristics of anti-Semitism in order to help detect and fight the old demon within our own ranks.

*History.* Beginning with the fourth century and lasting into the twentieth century, the history of anti-Semitism can be divided into four main phases or aspects.

1. The fourth century records the birth of anti-Semitism[5] in connection with the rejection of the law and the Sabbath, the first accusations of deicide, and the first teachings of supersessionism.

2. During the Middle Ages, at the time of the Crusades, anti-Semitism took a violent form for the first time. Massacres and pogroms became a part of the daily life of the Jews. Furthermore, medieval society forced the Jews to practice usury as the only profession allowed to them. From then on society associated Jews with money and even as the devil himself.

3. The nineteenth and twentieth centuries added a new ingredient to traditional anti-Semitism. Under the influence of anthropological and evolutionist studies, anti-Semitism developed into a racist theory that paved the way to the concentration camps and ultimately led to the Holocaust.

4. Since the Holocaust it has no longer been fashionable to be anti-Semitic. Yet anti-Semitism sometimes hides its face behind social and political justice and is then directed against the state of Israel. To be sure, not all who disagree with Israel's policies and politics are anti-Semitic. Otherwise, many Jews would

qualify. But the Arab-Israeli conflict has often become a pretext to vent and justify the old hatred. And many traits of the old ghost have reappeared. In the course of political argument some have identified Israelis with Nazis, a subtle way to minimize, justify, or simply ignore the reality of the Holocaust. Besides the traditional Christian anti-Semitism,[6] an Arab or pro-Arab anti-Semitism has emerged that has inherited most, if not all, of the Christian anti-Semitic myths and stereotypes.

*Psychological anti-Semitism.* A popular image of the Jew created and entertained in Christian circles includes that of a people of cupidity, wealth, and crass materialism. They are portrayed as having large noses, floppy ears, intimidating intelligence, and covetousness, and as being lovers of money. But even then the image of the Jew is always imprecise, out of focus, and varied according to the individuals, groups, and countries involved. Time and place also play a role in society's perception.

However, one point is constant: whatever may be the Jew's quality or fault, even when such traits occur among non-Jews Jews possess their faults or qualities only because they are Jewish. The hostility is often irrational.

This determination to be separate from the Jew almost seems to have been implanted in the Gentile subconsciousness. A terrible mark has been placed on the Jew's forehead—that of guilt. The difference, therefore, is not only on the plane of psychology. Anti-Semitism uses also the language of theology.

*Theological anti-Semitism.* In speaking of theological anti-Semitism, one assumes the reality of Christian anti-Semitism. But this often makes Christians uncomfortable. They do not want to think that they, who have been nurtured with the love of the gospel, are anti-Semitic or promote anti-Semitism. Yet further discussion often reveals concepts that they believe theologically justify Jewish suffering and persecution. "If the Jews have suffered so much through anti-Semitism, it is because—" Then follow explanations, theological arguments, and "reasons of conscience" that have through the centuries sent Jews to the stake and the scaffold. Some individuals may also explain murder and assassination as unfortunate necessities.

In short, the Jew in all ages, and even today, is considered to be responsible for the death of God—simply because 2,000 years ago some of his or her probable ancestors could have sentenced Jesus of Nazareth to be crucified. Anti-Semitism thus feeds on theological reproach.

This was perfectly clear to Søren Kierkegaard, who said: "Tell [to the child] the tribulations of Jesus during His life, the betrayal by one of His close companions, the denial by several others, the insults and revilings of others up to the very moment when they finally nailed Him to the cross, as you can see in the sacred pictures, asking that His blood fall on them and on their children, while He prayed for them and asked that this not be so, and that the heavenly Father would forgive their sin. . . . Tell how at the same time that Love lived, an infamous thief sentenced to die was preferred by the people who greeted his release with hurrahs . . . while they cried out: 'Crucify Him! Crucify Him!' in the face of Love. . . . What impression do you think that story will make on the child? . . . He will resolve firmly, when he has grown up, to cut to pieces the ungodly who acted thus toward Love." [7]

Something I saw on a television program in Austria during the Easter season several years ago confirmed to me Kierkegaard's observation. A former Nazi, now "repentant," explained how such indictment of the Jew had been taught to him repeatedly since his early youth and had contributed largely to instilling in him a hatred, even as an atheist, that would qualify him as a future member of the Hitler Youth.

Of course, not all German or Austrian Christians fell into the snares of Nazism. Many of them, even when they were anti-Semitic, battled this evil at the peril of their lives. Yet those same Christians who opposed the Nazi monster, possibly unconsciously and without understanding the consequences of their attitude, tried to explain, at least partially, the Jewish predicament.

Worse yet is the trick such reasoning can play on conscience. Persecution of the Jews actually becomes the will of God; thus one can be at peace in hatred, as well as in indifference.

Furthermore, the deicide theory not only encourages Christians in their hatred and scorn, but may also explain the Jewish refusal to engage in any discussion. "The more relentless Christians are in their accusation, the more stubborn Jews remain in their denial."[8]

All this information serves only one purpose: to enable our minds and our hearts to recognize and track down anti-Semitic feelings and thoughts and then neutralize them. We should learn to purify our words, our jokes, our sermons, and also our liturgical services from any kind of anti-Semitic traces. Most of all, we should learn to bring the good news to the world without having to make it bad news for the Jews.

First, we must begin with our theology of Israel by not

thinking, teaching, and preaching that God has rejected the Jews, that they are cursed, and that they have been replaced by the church, the very church (including the Adventist Church)[9] that persecuted them or would have persecuted them. This duty holds even within apologetic rhetoric against dispensationalism. To respond to the dispensationalists, who like to emphasize the blessings of Israel and its central place in prophecy, Adventist evangelists and theologians often fall into the other extreme and emphasize the curses against Israel and deny its people any place in God's plan of salvation. Thus in good religious conscience they have reanimated the old beast and all the anti-Semitic myths that produced the Holocaust. Also, in order to win evangelical Christians from dispensationalism, they lose along the way the Jews who may hear their anti-Semitic rhetoric. Such an approach reminds one of the first apostasy of the church, when it compromised with pagan idolatry in order to win the Gentiles, losing the Jews in the process.

Such a program of spiritual detoxification and reconciliation is heavy and difficult. Is it impossible? I do not know. I only know that Jewish-Christian reconciliation within Adventism, theological as well as human, is part of the prophetic role of Elijah. It is an absolute prerequisite for its mission to the Jews and, I am tempted to say, even for its mission to the world.

### 3. MISSION TO THE JEWS

We need to remember that the early successful Christian mission to the Jews collapsed essentially because of the Jewish-Christian separation. This lesson of history teaches us that the Christian mission to the Jews may recover its rights and its efficiency only when Christians relate differently to Jews, only when they will strive to "repair the breach" (see Isa. 58:12) and work at healing the 2,000-year-old wound.

As long as Adventists will not understand the part of their prophetic role that implies reconciliation and repentance—that is, a new attitude toward the Jews—the mission to the Jews is bound to fail. At times a rare conversion may occur, but there will never be a significant Jewish response to the Adventist message, as true as it may be, even with the Torah. You cannot bring the gospel of love and the testimony of Jesus to someone when hatred and prejudice haunt your mind and heart. Nor can you speak convincingly to a Jew (whether religious or secular) if in the back of your mind you think of him or her as a part of a "rejected" and "cursed" people, an attitude that, incidentally, you would not entertain as you approach a Buddhist or a Catholic. Such thinking and prejudice will precede your testimony like red flags in your words and your body language.

In other words, the prerequisite of Jewish-Christian reconciliation suggests a specific methodology for the mission to the Jews.

Instead of bringing Jesus to the Jews with the preconceived idea that they have been rejected and are guilty, hardened, and resistant to the gospel, share the gospel within the context of love, humility, and justice. Share the message of Jesus to the Jews in relation to the bringing of the law to the Christians. Jews will be more receptive to the truth of Jesus if this message has an accompanying call to Christians to come back to the Jewish roots they formerly rejected. This includes a summons for Christians to repent of anti-Semitism and to restore the divine law, including the Sabbath, in their teachings and their life.

What is happening today before our eyes seems to confirm this strategy. As many Christians move toward the Jews and are interested in refreshing their Jewish roots, we see on the other side for the first time many Jews willing to discover the Jewish heritage of Jesus.

It is interesting that after the Holocaust many Christian theologians, both Catholic and Protestant, have initiated a work of reconciliation between the church and Israel. The first effective Jewish-Christian dialogues and serious explorations of Jewish-Christian relations began in earnest only after the Holocaust and the creation of the state of Israel. Today Jewish and Christian organizations sponsor conferences and publications, maintain interfaith activities, and encourage research to deal with Jewish-Christian concerns. Leading Christian theologians are even ready in the wake of Jewish-Christian conversation to reconsider their theology of the law.[10] The movement has invaded the people at large. More and more Christians from all denominations find themselves fascinated and attracted by the Jewish face of their Christian identity. Many want to keep the seventh-day Sabbath (I am not referring here to Seventh-day Adventists), eat kosher, learn Hebrew, and worship in Jewish style. Christian sympathy for the Jews has never been so high.[11]

On the other hand, an interesting new phenomenon is also happening in Israel. Paradoxically, since Auschwitz and especially after the creation of the state of Israel, never in history have so many Jews been as open to the gospel as they are today.[12] More and more Jews, including leading Jewish theologians, are ready to reconsider their theology of incarnation[13] and the mystery of the Messiahship of Jesus.[14] And more and more Jews—religious and secular, rabbis and laypeople—are willing to read the Gospels and get acquainted with the person of Jesus. In the past 30 years Jews have written more about Jesus than they did during the previous two millennia. The growth of messianic Jews throughout the world, especially in the United States and Israel, is also a significant evidence of this movement.

The reason for this new phenomenon resides in a new Jewish perception of Jesus, including a new Christian emphasis on the Jewishness of Jesus and the experience of the state of Israel. This nation is a historical reality that testifies through its landscapes, its archaeological discoveries, and through the visits of Christian tourists in the Holy Land. For the first time in history Jews are recognizing Jesus as a part of their cultural heritage.[15] Before now the message of the gospel came as something foreign to the Jews, if not against them. No wonder it was never an option for them during this period of time. Paul's intriguing reference to the factor of jealousy in the mechanism of the conversion of the Jews and the Gentiles (Rom. 11:11, 14) makes sense only within that new paradigm. Jealousy can rise only when the other takes and enjoys something or someone we consider as ours. Jewish jealousy about Jesus is then possible insofar as Jesus is situated within the Jewish heritage. Only when Jews seek Jesus as a part of their legacy and in accordance with Jewish values and the Torah inherited from God will they be provoked to jealousy and therefore be susceptible to responding to the Christian testimony.[16]

I have personally learned the same lesson from my own experience as a witness. My writings and public "evangelistic" lectures throughout the world have dealt basically with Jewish-Christian reconciliation, and not directly with the mission to the Jews. The thrust of my messages, calling the Jews to recognize that Jesus is a legitimate part of their Jewish heritage and urging Christians to repent and come back to the law of

God testified by the Jews, has attracted many Jews and many Christians *alike*. From that perspective I have been able to communicate the truth about the Messiah to the Jews and the truth of the law and the Sabbath to Christians.

Such movements, both among Jews and Christians, suggest that in a certain sense the mission to the world is somewhat connected with the mission to the Jews. Indeed, it may well be that the mission to the Jews will affect the world mission scene. We do not know how events will play out and how the ultimate mission will proceed. At this stage we can only vaguely sense the current of history. The rest still belongs to the unfolding of prophecy.

## 4. ISRAEL IN PROPHECY

The biblical prophecy that is the most explicit and extensive about the future destiny of Israel appears in Hosea, a book concerned with God's covenant with His people Israel (Hosea 1; 2; 12:3, 4). When approached from the perspective of New Testament fulfillment, Hosea's prophecy about Israel suggests three phases:

The *first phase* applies to the first coming of Jesus and the rise of Christianity (Hosea 2:14-23; cf. John 17:3; Rom. 9:25, 26). It concerns first the same historical Israel who "shall sing . . . as in the days of her youth, and in the day when she came up from the land of Egypt" (Hosea 2:15) and with whom God will renew His covenant (verse 18). The relationship is symbolized as an experience of "betrothal" with God "in righteousness and justice, in lovingkindness and mercy" (verse 19). Under this new covenant the people will "know the Lord" (verse 20). Indeed, this text contains the promise that after the Captivity Israel would come back to the Promised Land and be replanted there (verses 21-23).

But beyond the return from exile (which would take place in the time of Old Testament Israel) the New Testament applies this prophecy to the events associated with the first coming of Jesus. It concerns the "many" Jews who accepted Jesus during His lifetime on earth and in early Christianity. We find this interpretation implied in Jesus' prayer describing the experience of His disciples who will "know the Lord" (John 17:3). It also concerns the other nations who will then enter the covenant and become God's people, an interpretation explicitly given by the apostle Paul, who applies Hosea's prophecy "I will say to those who were not My people, 'you are my people!'" (Hosea 2:23) to the integration of the Gentiles: "Even us whom He called, not of the Jews only, but also of the Gentiles" (Rom. 9:24). Likewise, Peter spoke of those "who once were not a people but are now the people of God" (1 Peter 2:10).

The *second phase,* a continuation of the first event, focuses also on the historical "Jewish" Israel that follows the renewal of the covenant.[17] The prophet describes God's relationship with Israel in these terms: "You shall stay with me many days, you shall not play the harlot, nor shall you have a man—so, too, will I be toward you" (Hosea 3:3). Note that the prophet does not portray the relationship between God and Jewish Israel in terms of rejection. They are still His people—He did not reject them, nor did He replace them. Instead God commits Himself to them: "So, too, will I be toward you" (verse 3). This phase applies to the Jews during the two millennia when they would not have access to the good news of the gospel, essentially because of the apostasy *and the oppression* of the church. During this time they remained without a king, without theocracy, and without prophecy, but were still God's chosen witness.

The *third phase* is eschatological and still involves the same historical "Jewish" Israel in the latter days *(acharit ha-yammim):* "Afterward the children of Israel shall return and seek the Lord their God and David their king. They shall fear the Lord and His goodness in the latter days" (verse 5). The prophet sees in this Israel a movement of "return," a *teshuva* that will take place at the end of time. Paul in Romans 11 seems to endorse this prophecy, since he also foresees a future grafting of "natural branches" (Rom. 11:24).[18]

Indeed, if we apply the prophecy of Hosea 2:14–23 to the rise of Christianity as the New Testament writers do, we should be consistent and also apply the following prophecy of Hosea 3 to the history that comes *after* the rise of Christianity until the end of times. The conclusion of the passage further supports such an interpretation, since it concerns precisely the time of the end: "Afterward the children of Israel shall return and seek the Lord their God and David their king. They shall fear the Lord and His goodness in the latter days" (Hosea 3:5). The language is clearly messianic ("David their king") and eschatological ("in the latter days"; see Isa. 2:2, 3; Gen. 49:1; Num. 24:14; Dan. 10:14). Also, the parallel text of Ezekiel 37, which uses the same lexical and thematic association ("return of Israel" [see verse 21] to "the future king David" [see verses 24, 25]), brings the perspective of the messianic era, when an everlasting covenant of peace will be made (verse 26). "[God's] tabernacle will be with them," and "the nations also will know . . . the Lord" (verses 27, 28) under the rule of David, "their prince forever" (verse 25). This intertextual observation provides from within the Hebrew Scriptures enough clues to support the messianic and eschatological interpretation of the prophetic passage in Hosea 3.

Some may even wonder exactly to what extent the state of Israel does not, or will not, play some part in the prophetic game. Adventist theologians have been so afraid of the dispensationalist temptation that they have totally excluded any possible prophetic application for Israel, thus throwing the baby out with the bathwater. Personally I think that the tie is too thin and the evidence too vague to be able to establish or elaborate a clear and solid theological case. But in matters of prophetic interpretation we must learn to remain humble, prudent, and open. Remember that before the creation of the state of Israel a great number of Adventist theologians had speculated and made eloquent declarations that the Jews would never reoccupy Palestine. We know now how wrong they were.

Abraham Heschel's positive yet prudent observation is worth noting: "The state of Israel is not the fulfillment of the messianic promise, but it makes the messianic promise plausible." [19] Indeed, the state of Israel not only has created a society free from anti-Semitism, thus liberating the Jew from the anti-Christian reflex of suspicion, but also has exposed the Jew in *Eretz Israel* to the Jewishness of the Jesus of history. One could interpret the creation of the state of Israel as a miracle and even suppose that this event may play a role in the prophecy of the conversion of the Jews, and yet not fall into the dispensationalist trap. Our sympathy (or antipathy) for Israel should not lead us astray and affect our prophetic interpretation of the biblical text. The need for prophecy should not make prophecy.

One thing remains certain, however, and that is the fact that the ultimate progress of conversion will take place within the walls of the Seventh-day Adventist "movement," for two reasons. The first we have already singled out: the theological identity of the Seventh-day Adventist Church, which is the only formal religious entity that has reunited the law and Jesus and presents the "gospel . . . in its fulness."[20] It is the only one, therefore, entitled and capable of reaching out to the two witnesses. The second we have implicitly stated: the prophetic identity of this church. The Seventh-day Adventist movement did not merely arise for reconciliation purposes to bring *shalom* between Jews and Christians and recover the original connection between Torah and Jesus. Nor is it just the natural heir of the two historic Israels, the cultural product of a historical process. In addition to working on reconciliation and learning from the two witnesses, we as eschatological Israel have also received a unique message that has not been, and still is not being, witnessed to by the two others. Seventh-day Adventism is a "prophetic" movement, not just because biblical prophecy announced its rise and message, or because it attests to a prophetic experience through Ellen G. White, but, without excluding all of the above, because it carries a testimony that concerns the future. The vocation of the Seventh-day Adventist Church is not of a historical order alone, or to remind us of past events or to inspire present existence. It also has an eschatological role—to proclaim the future event of salvation and to play a decisive role in "the closing proclamation of the gospel."[21] In that sense the Seventh-day Adventist Church identifies itself differently than a mere witness who has seen and remembers—it regards itself as a sign pointing to something beyond itself, elsewhere and in the future. It is prophetic by nature.

---

[1] On this, see Jacques Doukhan, *Secrets of Revelation: The Apocalypse Through Hebrew Eyes* (Hagerstown, Md.: Review and Herald Pub. Assn., 2002), pp. 123-138.

[2] On the Jewish influence on Christian reform movements, see Louis Israel Newman, *Jewish Influence on Christian Reform Movements* (New York: Columbia University Press, 1925).

[3] See Ellen White's comments: "In this time . . . God calls upon His messengers to proclaim His law. . . . As John the Baptist, in preparing a people for Christ's advent, called their attention to the Ten Commandments, so we are to give, with no uncertain sound, the message: 'Fear God, and give glory to him; for the hour of his judgment is come.' With the earnestness that characterized Elijah the prophet and John the Baptist, we are to strive to prepare the way for Christ's second advent (*Southern Watchman,* Mar. 21, 1905)" (*The Seventh-day Adventist Bible Commentary,* Ellen G. White Comments, vol. 4, p. 1184).

[4] On the name "Seventh-day Adventist," Ellen White comments on the basis of Revelation 14:12 that it is "a distinctive" name that adequately describes the ideal of the remnant people of God. They have both the commandments of God and the faith of Jesus. "This is the Law and the gospel," she writes (*Selected Messages,* book 2, p. 385). In another passage dealing again with the choice of the name "Seventh-day Adventist," she explains that it expresses "the peculiar and prominent features of their faith," namely, "the observance of the seventh day and waiting for the appearing of the Lord from heaven" (*Testimonies,* vol. 1, p. 223). A few lines further she again insists that "the name of Seventh-day Adventist carries the true features of our faith in front," which she explicitly identifies as "God's law" and "our Lord Jesus Christ" (p. 224).

[5] See James W. Parkes, *The Conflict of the Church and the Synagogue: A Study in the Origins of Antisemitism* (Cleveland: World Pub. Co., 1961), pp. 153-195; Marc Saperstein, *Moments of Crisis in Jewish-Christian Relations* (Philadelphia: Trinity Press International, 1989), pp. 7-13.

[6] See Phyllis Chesler, *The New Anti-Semitism: The Current Crisis and What We Must Do About It* (Jossey-Bass Pub. Co., 2003); cf. Gabriel Schoenfeld, *The Return of Anti-Semitism* (San Francisco: Encounter Books, 2004).

[7] Søren Kierkegaard, *Training in Christianity and the Edifying Discourse Which "Accompanied" It,* trans. with intro. and notes by Walter Lowrie (Princeton, N.J.: Princeton University Press, 1944), pp. 176-178. For Kierkegaard, Christian pedagogy must on the contrary make the child understand his or her own culpability in the Crucifixion. Moreover, he says explicitly, "This present generation must think that they themselves have crucified Him."

[8] Jules Isaac, *Jesus and Israel,* ed. Claire H. Bishop, trans. Sally Gran (New York: Holt, Rinehart and Winston, 1971), p. 386.

[9] On Adventist theology after Auschwitz and the role of the Adventist Church during the Holocaust, see Jacques Doukhan, ed., *Thinking in the Shadow of Hell: The Impact of the Holocaust on Theology and Jewish-Christian*

*Relations* (Berrien Springs, Mich.: Andrews University Press, 2002).

[10] See Catholic Hans Küng, in *Explorations* (Philadelphia: The Institute, 1992), vol. 6, no. 2, and Protestant Clark M. Williamson, *A Guest in the House of Israel: Post-Holocaust Church Theology* (Louisville, Ky.: Westminster/John Knox Press, 1993), pp. 123-125. See also the "Restore Movement" or the Jewish Roots Movement, which affect all branches of Christianity.

[11] It is a movement that is to be commended. On the other hand, we have to be cautious in regard to "Gentile" Christians who suddenly pretend they are Jewish when in fact they are absolutely not. This curious and recent phenomenon has surfaced in both Adventist and dispensationalist circles in which mystical ideas about the Jews have developed (they fulfill some prophecy or other). Such "new" Jews therefore generally get recruited from among mystics and extremists. Both dispensationlists and Adventists have used this self-identification as a missionary strategy to reach out to the Jews. Needless to say, the ethical issues raised by such cases should urge us toward caution. Such false claims are not only deceitful; they also sometimes involve strange and dangerous behavior (exorcism, Messiah syndrome, financial exploitation, etc.). In addition, such practices ultimately compromise the true mission to the true Jews and turn God's call into just a farce.

[12] See Schalom Ben-Chorin, *Bruder Jesus: Der Nazarener in jüdischer Sicht* (Munich: List, 1967); Samuel Sandmel, *We Jews and Jesus* (New York: Oxford University Press, 1973); Géza Vermès, *The Gospel of Jesus the Jew* (Newcastle upon Tyne: University of Newcastle upon Tyne, 1981); David Flusser, *Jesus* (New York: Herder and Herder, 1969); Joseph Klausner and Herbert Danby, *Jesus of Nazareth: His Life, Times, and Teaching* (New York: Macmillan, 1943); Pinchas E. Lapide, *Der Rabbi von Nazaret: Wandlungen des jüdischen Jesusbildes* (Trier: Spee-Verlag, 1974); Donald A. Hagner, *The Jewish Reclamation of Jesus: An Analysis and Critique of Modern Jewish Study of Jesus* (Grand Rapids: Academie Books, 1984).

[13] See Michael Wyschogrod, "A Jewish View of Christianity," in *Toward a Theological Encounter: Jewish Understandings of Christianity,* ed. Leon Klenicki (New York: Paulist Press, 1991), pp. 106-119.

[14] See Arthur W. Kac, ed., *The Messiahship of Jesus: Are Jews Changing Their Attitude Toward Jesus?* (Grand Rapids: Baker Book House, 1980).

[15] See especially Hagner, *The Jewish Reclamation of Jesus.*

[16] Interestingly, Ellen White confirms this missiological methodology and emphasizes that Paul never proclaimed "to the Jews a Messiah whose work is to destroy the old dispensation, but a Messiah who came to develop the whole Jewish economy in accordance with the truth" (*Evangelism* [Washington, D.C.: Review and Herald Pub. Assn., 1946], p. 554). Likewise, concerning the future conversion of many Jews at the time of the end, she points out that

they will see "the Christ of the gospel dispensation portrayed in the pages of the Old Testament Scriptures" (*The Acts of the Apostles,* p. 381).

[17] See White, *Prophets and Kings,* p. 298.

[18] *Ibid.*

[19] Abraham Heschel, *Israel: An Echo of Eternity* (New York: Farrar, Straus and Giroux, 1969), p. 223.

[20] "When this gospel shall be presented in its fullness to the Jews," says Ellen White, "many will accept Christ as the Messiah" (*The Acts of the Apostles,* p. 380).

[21] *Ibid.,* p. 381.

# What, Then, Is Israel?

The answer to that question cannot be simple. The complex picture of Israel and its theological identification in the prophetic documents, the fluctuations and surprises of history, and the variety of theological proposals have made a clear definition of Israel extremely difficult to formulate. The data suggest, however, the following reality of a multiplicity of faces of "Israel" as God's chosen people.

First, "biblical Israel" was born of the descendants of the patriarch Jacob/Israel and joined, through marriage or spiritual adoption, to peoples from other nations: Egyptians (Ex. 12:38, 39), Midianites (Ex. 18:1), Cushites (Num. 12:1), Canaanites (Joshua 2:1), Moabites (Ruth 1:16, 17), Persians (Esther 9:27), Arameans (Job 1:1), and so forth. As we can see, it was not a people of pure, or unmixed, lineage. The notion of "pure lineage" developed late in the human consciousness and was invented in the course of the racist theories of the nineteenth century and later exploited in Nazi ideology. "Biblical Israel" testified to God and to the history of salvation, and was called "Israel" by the prophets and by God, who loved His people "with an everlasting love" (Jer. 31:2, 3). The situation remained the same in New Testament times when proselytes joined the community of Israel through the testimony of the Pharisees (Matt. 23:15) and later the early Christians (Acts 13:43).

Second, "Jewish Israel" consists of the community of Jews who survived the exile of Babylon and settled around Eastern and Western Europe (probably Ashkenazic Jews), as well as those who fled Palestine after the fall of Jerusalem and settled around the Mediterranean (probably Sephardic Jews). These peoples are not any purer than the biblical version of Israel. Many peoples from European and Mediterranean countries also joined this community of faith (see the stories of conversion to Judaism in France during the Middle Ages, in Russia with the Khazars, and in pre-Islamic Arab countries). This "Israel" survived in order to witness in the flesh and in teaching the Torah of God, the expression of God's will and character.

This "Israel" has preserved cultural as well as spiritual roots with "biblical Israel" by keeping the Hebrew language and Hebrew Scriptures alive through regular studies and liturgical services, preserving a physical relationship with "biblical Israel" through observing the rituals of circumcision, and continuing such cultural traditions as the Talith, ancient prayers, rites of eating and drinking, and the observance of festivals. Besides its cultural identity, this Israel has developed a psychological identity as a result of common sufferings and oppressions. Anti-Semitism has also shaped the Jewish identity.[1] However, because of the "failure" of the Christian witness, the Jewish witness has not been able to learn about another important aspect of its legitimate heritage, namely, the person, the teaching, and the ministry of salvation of Jesus the Messiah. And yet God did not reject the Jewish people. Paul is clear about it (Rom. 11:1), and

Ellen White emphasizes: "Even though Israel rejected His Son, God did not reject them."[2] Since the coming of Christ this Israel remains without king, prophet, or theocracy, and yet still is God's witness to the Torah. It is significant that Ellen White still describes the Jewish people of that period of time in relation to God as "His commandment-keeping people."[3]

Within this cultural and historical context belongs the political Israel, created in 1948 on the ashes of the Holocaust. This Israel may be considered essentially as a political and cultural entity with no theocratic or prophetic claim whatsoever. It participates in, however, the same witnessing vocation as "Jewish Israel"—witnessing historically to the Torah, the Sabbath, the Hebrew Scriptures, and culture and salvation history as it occurred in *Eretz Israel* (the land of Israel). Political Israel is also a compound figure, incorporating peoples from a great variety of cultural, ethnic, and geographical horizons: European Jews, Arab Jews, Ethiopian Jews, Indian Jews, Yemenite Jews, Russian-Mongol Jews, African Jews, even Chinese Jews, to whom new converts are increasingly joining from various backgrounds.

Third, "Christian Israel" is descendant by birth of the early Jewish Christians, but also, and more important, by conversions through the intense evangelistic and political activities of Christians throughout the world. It has witnessed to the event of Jesus Christ, to His teachings and example. Also, through the testimony about the Jesus born in Israel and about the Gospels and the New Testament, Christian Israel has been culturally and historically related to "biblical Israel," being nurtured by the same stories and teachings. For this reason Christian Israel can also claim a place in the house of Israel, an idea taught in Jewish tradition.[4] As Jewish Orthodox theologian Rabbi Irving

Greenberg observes: "Only Christians . . . may be deemed to be members of the people Israel, even as they practice differing religions than Jewry does."[5] The grafting, however, has suffered amputation since the church has consciously rejected its connection with its Jewish identification, as well as the Torah, and created a new cultural identity of its own, distinct from "Jewish Israel." However, it is an interesting irony and paradox that in spite of the church's betrayal of its roots, it is through the "universalistic" testimony of "Christian Israel" that the people of Israel, the Jews, have been made known to the world. If it were not for the Christian testimony, Judaism would have remained a small and obscure sect that might well have disappeared. "Christian Israel," like the other Israel, is also a mixed people made up of all cultures and nations with one exception—the Jewish people, which have been excluded as a result of the phenomena of rejection that we have been examining.[6]

Fourth, "eschatological Israel" has developed from a movement of return *(Teshuvah)* toward the ideal represented by "biblical Israel" and has separated itself from traditional "Christian Israel" in that it reclaimed the testimony about the Torah along with the testimony about Jesus. Therefore, this Israel is open not only to Christians but also to Jews and transcends both cultural communities. It is a movement summoned at the end of time to bring the "light of present truth" and prepare the world for the kingdom of God.[7]

---

[1] Jean-Paul Sartre, *Anti-Semite and Jew,* trans. George J. Becker (New York: Schocken Books, 1972), pp. 95, 143.

[2] E. G. White, *The Acts of the Apostles,* p. 375.

[3] White, *Prophets and Kings,* p. 299.

[4] See, for instance, Maimonides' teaching about Christianity at the end of his great code *Mishneh Torah,* in which he recognizes that in spite of their er-

rors Christians are the instruments of Providence, since they brought all humanity to the worship of the one true God (ironically, the Christian censors of the printed version of *Mishneh Torah* forced the publishers to remove the passage). Furthermore, in a response written after the publication of *Mishneh Torah*, Maimonides rules that Christians are the only community of faith to whom Jews could teach Torah, for Jews and Christians share a common revelation in a unique way (versus the Muslims, whose primary text is the Koran). See David Novak, "The Mind of Maimonides," *First Things* 90 (February 1999): 27-33.

[5] Irving Greenberg, "Judaism and Christianity: Covenants of Redemption," in *Christianity in Jewish Terms,* ed. Tikva Frymer-Kensky et al., p. 158.

[6] Even if Christian theology does not accept this exclusion, it remains a historical fact that Jews have not responded to the gospel. Their conversions have been rare throughout the history of the church.

[7] See White, *Evangelism,* p. 578.

# Conclusion

We should conclude with God's dream for Israel—His theology of Israel.

For there is still another Israel to consider, the only one that counts—the "heavenly Israel" in the New Jerusalem. The only Israel that will survive the dust of human history, it is the "saved Israel," the "remnant" found in all the above Israels but that also transcends all of them, the "all Israel." This is the "new Israel," the "spiritual Israel," the "144,000," the "great multitude." No group presently on earth has the right to call itself by this new name. Only God will identify and label the "new Israel" (Gen. 32:28; Rev. 2:17; 3:12; 21:10). And only He has the right and the power to decide and judge who is rejected or who is not (Dan. 7:9, 10). He will decide on the basis of His mercy and on the basis of what He knows, and also on the basis of what we have been able to hear (Rom. 10:14). It is the Israel that is in God's mind, in that sense perhaps the "Israel of God." All the other "Israels" are historical Israels that fulfill a particular mission. As such, none of them can or should claim to be more Israel—more the "Israel of God"—than any of the others. To belong to a religious community or to a people does not give anyone the right of spiritual or ethnic superiority, and it is not enough to belong to that community to thereby claim to belong to the "saved" "new Israel." Also, according to the biblical view of anthropology, it must be said that the members of all these "Israels" are Israel of the flesh, including those who have spiritually or culturally joined that community. Even though we are of the flesh, we are entitled to be also of the Spirit, and conversely, when we are of the Spirit, we exist in our flesh. There is no dissociation between flesh and Spirit. And in heaven the new Israel will be Israel both in Spirit and flesh, only this time fully so.

Only then will "the mystery" fulfill its real meaning and become revelation. "For now we see in a mirror, dimly, but then face to face. Now I know in part, but then I shall know just as I also am known" (1 Cor. 13:12). In the meantime, the essential conclusion drawn for us from this humble recognition is the following: "And now abide faith, hope, love, these three; but the greatest of these is love" (verse 13).

# Ellen White and the Jews

## INTRODUCTION
## PROBLEMS AND METHODS

The impact of Ellen White's writings on Seventh-day Adventist theology is significant enough to justify a careful examination of her writings and thus develop a healthy Seventh-day Adventist theology of Israel.

It is interesting and certainly highly significant that most (if not all) the works devoted to the topic of Israel or the Jews in Ellen White's writings have focused mainly on the mission toward the Jews. We have neglected altogether theological questions concerning the meaning of Israel and the Jews, ethical and philosophical questions involving Christian anti-Semitism, and practical questions related to that very mission.

Furthermore, it is also our observation that Seventh-day Adventists have often employed her writings to support their own views or even their personal biases regarding the Jews and Israel, especially their theology of rejection.

Certainly the present study will not settle the dispute. Texts—especially sacred ones—are often subject to a variety of interpretations, depending on the aspect one wishes to emphasize. And probably our investigation will not escape such criticism. But that should not discourage us. Our intention is not to force this interpretation over another one, but rather to humbly show that there exist other texts and other perspectives to consider—other readings that would call for a cautious and more nuanced and balanced handling of her writings.

For that purpose we will not content ourselves with simply collecting all the passages dealing with the subject. Too often people have selected and used Ellen White's writings outside their respective context without taking the pains to explore and analyze what *she really meant*.

We will, therefore, conduct our study as a reflective and exegetical essay about what Ellen White wrote on Israel and the Jews. It will not only take into consideration the literary and historical context of the various passages, but also decode her words and language so that we may understand as much as possible the meaning she herself intended to convey.

It appears that Ellen White's thinking about Israel revolves around four main issues: (1) Israel's rejection of God; (2) God's rejection of Israel; (3) eschatological prophecies about Israel and the Jews; and (4) the mission to the Jews. Our exposition and discussion of Ellen White's writings will develop along these four axes and will infer from them the theological, prophetic, and missiological lessons we need to learn about Israel and the Jews.

## THE REJECTION OF GOD

The first and most fundamental question concerns the nature of Jewish responsibility in the crucifixion of Christ and, by implication, the question of whether the Jews as a people are guilty of having rejected God. To this basic question Ellen White consistently gives the same clear and unambiguous answer:

## 1. The Jewish Leaders Were Responsible for the Crucifixion.

"The sin of the priests and rulers was greater than that of any preceding generation. By their rejection of the Savior, they were making themselves *responsible* for the blood of all the righteous men slain from Abel to Christ." [1]

Note that the term *responsible* does not apply to the people in a collective sense. Instead, it specifically refers to "the priests and rulers." It is also interesting and indeed significant that she no longer associates these "priests and rulers" with the particular category of Israel—they now belong to the more general class of those who slew the righteous, including those who existed even before Israel ("from Abel . . ."). She does not condemn them as "wicked Jews" but as "wicked men" who from the beginning of human history have perpetrated murders and iniquity. We find the intention of this association confirmed in another passage in which Ellen White identifies the same Jewish leaders with today's "professed followers of Christ":

"Shall the warnings of God be passed by unheeded? Shall the opportunities for service be unimproved? Shall the world's scorn, the pride of reason, conformity to human customs and traditions, hold the professed *followers of Christ* from service to Him? Will they reject God's Word as the Jewish *leaders* rejected Christ?" [2]

On the consequences of this crime, namely, the rejection of God Himself, Ellen White is no less clear.

## 2. The Priests and the Leaders Were Those Who Rejected God.

"The Jewish rulers did not love God; therefore they cut

themselves away from Him, and rejected all His overtures for a just settlement."[3]

Then commenting on the parable of the vineyard, Ellen White develops the same lesson and clearly identifies the priests and the Jewish leaders as the husbandmen of the parable of the vineyard who "reject the Holy One of Israel":

"Christ, the Beloved of God, came to assert the claims of the Owner of the vineyard; but the *husbandmen* treated Him with marked contempt, saying, We will not have this man to rule over us. They envied Christ's beauty of character. His manner of teaching was far superior to theirs, and they dreaded His success. He remonstrated with them, unveiling their hypocrisy, and showing them the sure results of their course of action. This stirred them to madness. They smarted under the rebukes they could not silence. They hated the high standard of righteousness which Christ continually presented. They saw that His teaching was placing them where their selfishness would be uncloaked, and they determined to kill Him. They hated His example of truthfulness and piety and the elevated spirituality revealed in all He did. His whole life was a reproof to their selfishness, and when the final test came, the test which meant obedience unto eternal life or disobedience unto eternal death, they rejected the Holy One of Israel. When they were asked to choose between Christ and Barabbas, they cried out, 'Release unto us Barabbas!' (Luke 23:18). 'Shall I crucify your King?' Pilate asked, and from the *priests and rulers* came the answer, 'We have no king but Caesar' (John 19:15)."[4]

Indeed, for Ellen White the husbandmen of the vineyard are the Jewish leaders and not the people, since she referred to them as those who teach and were jealous of Jesus' success among the people. After this explicit identification, "the Jewish rulers" at the beginning of the quotation become "the husbandmen" who are from then on referred to with the simple personal pronoun "they." She uses the pronoun throughout the passage as the direct subject of the act of rejection. "They envied Christ . . ." "They smarted under the rebukes . . ." "They could not silence . . ." "They hated [His] high standard of righteousness . . ." "They saw that His teaching . . ." "They determined to kill Him." "They hated His example . . ." "They rejected the Holy One . . ." "They cried out . . ." And last, at the end of the quotation, she explicitly identifies them again. "From the priests and rulers came the answer . . ." In fact, in another quotation, just one page before, Ellen White labeled the husbandmen of the parable of the vineyard as the leaders and the priests. "The husbandmen who had been placed in charge of the Lord's vineyard were untrue to their trust. The priests and teachers were not faithful instructors of the people."[5] And again she repeats the same identification: "In the parable of the vineyard, after Christ had portrayed before the priests their crowning act of wickedness" "they saw in the husbandmen a picture of themselves."[6] From this we see that Ellen White draws the logical distinction between the Jewish people, as such, and their leaders.

## 3. The Jewish Leaders Were Distinct From the Jewish People.

This distinction is already implicit in the way Ellen White describes the "ignorant mob" accompanying the Jewish leaders as they cried together, "His blood be on us, and our children."[7] It is furthermore significant that in the sentence immediately following she specified that "thus the Jewish leaders made their choice,"[8] as if they remained alone to bear the guilt. As for the few ordinary Jews present with the Jewish leaders, she refers to them as ignorant, misinformed, and deceived by their superiors. Elsewhere she comments that "Peter urged home upon the convicted people the fact that they had rejected Christ because they had been deceived by the priests and rulers."[9]

In another passage that deals with the same issue, Ellen White presents the Jewish people involved in the Crucifixion as the victims of a plot initiated by Satan himself, who used the leaders for that purpose. It is interesting that she still makes a clear distinction between the two camps: Christ and the ordinary people on one side, and Satan and the Jewish leaders on the other.

"As Christ sought to place truth before the people in its proper relation to their salvation, Satan worked through the *Jewish leaders,* and inspired them with enmity against the Redeemer of the world. They determined to do all in their power to prevent Him from making an impression *upon the people.*"[10]

## THE REJECTION OF ISRAEL

Ellen White's declaration about the rejection of Israel is clear: Even though Israel spurned His Son, God did not abandon them.[11] Note that the phrase "God did not reject them" applies to the same Israel who "rejected His Son" and does not refer therefore to an ideal spiritual remnant, namely, the "good" Christians. It concerns the "bad" Jews; God did not cast them off in spite of their rejection. And yet she observes a few lines further: "Through unbelief and the rejection of Heaven's purpose for her, Israel as a nation had lost her connection with God."[12]

In the same manner she comments on the parable of the fig tree: "The parable of the unfruitful tree represented God's dealings with the Jewish nation. The command had gone forth, 'Cut it down; why cumbereth it the ground?' " [13] How can we reconcile these two seemingly contradictory statements? On the one hand, Ellen White affirms that God had not rejected Israel, the Jews as a people, in spite of their "stumbling" at the Crucifixion. On the other hand, she insists that the Jewish nation was the major object of God's rejection. We find the answer to that question through Ellen White's own terminology, more particularly the language she uses when she refers to the Jews who have been rejected. It is the duty of the interpreter who wishes to take seriously her message to go beyond the mere surface content of her words, to interpret their respective contexts and decode her language. Only then will we be able to understand what she really meant and thus solve what at first glance appears to be a contradiction.

## WHAT ELLEN WHITE MEANT BY "JEWISH NATION"

A careful attention to the passages that contain the expression "Jewish nation" reveals that Ellen White has in mind the leadership, the political entity with its theocratic claim.

The passages we have quoted above already imply this intention. The context of our last passage from *The Great Controversy* points to the Jewish rulers. She explicitly mentions the "Jewish leaders" in the preceding paragraph, as well as in the paragraph that follows, in which we find the expression "the rulers of the people." [14] It is also significant that Ellen White applies the divine rejection ("cut it down") to the "Jewish nation." She consistently uses the phrase "Jewish nation" as the equivalent and even a synonym for the Jewish leadership. Note, for instance, how she parallels the two expressions in the following quotation:

"'O Jerusalem, Jerusalem, thou that killest the prophets.' . . . This was the most solemn denunciation ever uttered against Jerusalem. After denouncing the hypocrisy of the *Jewish leaders,* who, while they worshiped the Temple, were working with a hatred inspired by Satan to destroy the only One who made the Temple sacred, Christ bade adieu to the once hallowed courts. . . . Thus with power and authority our Lord reproved the *Jewish nation.* 'Ye shall not see me henceforth.'"[15]

"In the son who said, 'I go, sir,' and went not, the character of the Pharisees was revealed. Like this son, the Jewish leaders were impenitent and self-sufficient. The religious life of the *Jewish nation* had become a pretense. . . . Had the conversion of the *Jews* been genuine, they would have received this testimony of John, and accepted Jesus as the Messiah, the One to whom all their sacrificial offerings pointed, and who was the foundation of all their economy."[16]

And immediately afterward she becomes more precise: "But *the Pharisees and the Sadducees* did not produce the fruits of repentance and sanctification and righteousness. They were of the class who said, 'I go, sir,' but went not."[17]

The identification of the Jewish nation with the Jewish leadership becomes clear as she makes a clear distinction between the people on the one hand and the nation itself and its leaders on the other hand.

"As He neared the time of separation from His disciples, His teaching became more significant and mysterious to their minds. He presented Himself before the people as the bread of life. The multitude were impressed with His teaching, large crowds followed Him, and precious rays of light were shed upon them; but the disciples no longer held to the hope that the Jews, as a *nation,* would receive Christ." [18]

"When Christ came to speak the words of life, the *common people* heard Him gladly; and many, even of the priests and rulers, believed on Him. But the *chief of the priesthood* and the *leading men of the nation* were determined to condemn and repudiate His teachings. . . . It was the influence of such teachers that led the Jewish nation to reject their Redeemer." [19]

As Ellen G. White used the expression "Jewish nation," she had in mind the Jewish leaders—the elites who functioned as its government in league with the Roman occupation—and not the Jews as a whole people. When she speaks of the rejection of the Jewish nation, it is only the political entity, the leadership, that is implied. The rest, on the other hand, still remain "the chosen people." Focusing on the event that took place at the end of the 70 weeks, at the time of the martyrdom of Stephen, she makes then a clear distinction between these two entities:

"The seventy weeks, or 490 years, especially allotted to the Jews, ended, as we have seen, in A.D. 34. At that time, through the action of the *Jewish Sanhedrin, the nation* sealed its rejection of the gospel by the martyrdom of Stephen and the persecution of the followers of Christ. Then the message of salvation, no longer restricted to *the chosen people,* was given to the world." [20]

It is noteworthy that Ellen White does not describe the fulfillment of the 70-weeks prophecy in negative terms of rejection, but in positive terms, as "the message of salvation," and a few lines further as "glad tidings." We find no mention whatsoever of a broken covenant. She does not present this crucial moment as a threat and a dreadful judgment against the Jewish people as a whole. According to Ellen White, the rejection concerns only the leadership, "the Jewish Sanhedrin" that is identified as "the nation." For the rest, she records this fulfillment as a great moment of hope for the salvation of other peoples in addition to, not in the place of, the "chosen people." The covenant continues with the chosen people and now broadens to the world.

## WHAT ELLEN WHITE MEANT BY "RACE OF THE JEWS"

Everyone knows now that the idea of a Jewish race is a dangerous and deceitful myth concocted in the nineteenth century in the wake of evolutionist theories. There is no Jewish race. And yet Ellen White uses this unfortunate expression.

"The Jews who first started the rage of the heathen against Jesus were not to escape. In the judgment hall the infuriated Jews cried, as Pilate hesitated to condemn Jesus, His blood be on us and on our children. The *race of the Jews* experienced the fulfillment of this terrible curse which they called down upon their own heads. . . . I saw that God had forsaken the *Jews as a nation.*"[21]

The context of this passage sheds light on the meaning of the particular term *race of the Jews.* In the beginning of the quotation Ellen White clearly identifies the Jews she has in mind. "The Jews who first started the rage of the heathen against Jesus." They are the Jews located "in the judgment hall" and who cried to Pilate, "His blood be on us . . . ." On the next page she specified that God's judgment concerns the "Jews as a nation" and not "Jews" as people, as the term *race of the Jews* may suggest. It is also particularly significant that in her book *Early Writings,* compiled a few years later, she corrected the quotation, replacing the phrase "the race of the Jews" with "the Jewish nation."

"The Jews who first aroused the rage of the heathen against Jesus were not to escape unpunished. In the judgment hall, as Pilate hesitated to condemn Jesus, the infuriated Jews cried, 'His blood be on us, and on our children.' The fulfillment of this terrible curse which they called down upon their own heads, the *Jewish nation* has experienced. . . . I saw that God had forsaken the Jews as a nation."[22]

The fact that she altered the expression "race of the Jews" to read "Jewish nation" indicates that the author realized that others might misunderstand it. And the fact that she changed the phrase into "Jewish nation" and that she judged the correction necessary at all suggests that in her mind the two expressions refer to two different entities.

The problem becomes even more complex as Ellen White often uses the general term *Jews* in a negative sense, having in mind more specifically the Jewish leaders. The context of our passage implies this sense. Likewise, in the following passage the "Scribes and Pharisees" are distinct from "the people" (other Jews), yet she also designates them as "the Jews."

"'Woe unto you, scribes and Pharisees, hypocrites!' . . . These fearful denunciations were made upon the Jews, because, while teaching the law of God to the people, they were not doers of the Word."[23]

In those passages the author employed the term *Jews* not in an ethnic sense but in a generic one to designate those who first initiated the Crucifixion, those who consciously rejected Him, namely, the Jewish leadership of Jerusalem.

## THE CURSE ON THE JEWS

The most important passage on the curse appears in *Early Writings*. Although we have already examined it, it deserves our further attention, for it is a key text often quoted to support the idea of an everlasting curse upon the Jews.

"The Jews who first aroused the rage of the heathen against Jesus were not to escape unpunished. In the judgment hall, as Pilate hesitated to condemn Jesus, the infuriated Jews cried, 'His blood be on us, and on our children.' The fulfillment of this terrible curse which they called down upon their own heads, the *Jewish nation* experienced. . . . They were degraded, shunned, and detested, *as if the brand of Cain* were upon them. Yet I saw that God had *marvelously preserved this people* and scattered them over the world that they might be looked upon as *specially visited by the curse of God*. I saw that God had forsaken the Jews as a nation." [24]

First, the context of the passage reveals that it focuses on the Jewish leadership. In addition, she uses the expression "nation" twice in the text. The passage starts with a reference to the Jews who "were not to escape unpunished" and who cried, "His blood be on us, and on our children." The next sentence explains the target of the curse: "The fulfillment of this terrible curse which they called down upon their own heads, the Jewish nation experienced." So the curse concerns the Jewish leaders, in other words, what she calls the "Jewish nation." We find this interpretation confirmed in another passage in which Ellen White associates the doom of the "Jewish nation" with the wickedness of the priests and other national leaders.

"In the parable of the vineyard, after Christ had portrayed before the priests their crowning act of wickedness," "unwittingly they had pronounced their own doom. . . . Christ would have averted the doom of the Jewish nation if the people had received Him. But envy and jealousy made them implacable. . . . The doom foretold came upon the Jewish nation." [25]

This passage concerns the Jewish leadership—the priests and rulers. The word "priests" occurs in our passage in connection with the technical expression "Jewish nation." Moreover, the allusion to the envy and the jealousy of this group shows that she has in mind the priests and the rulers *(the nation)*.

Also, concerning Jesus' parable of the barren fig tree, Ellen White implies that the "Jewish nation" has been cut down just like the tree. Here also the curse and the rejection specifically concerns the Jewish leaders, as the context clearly indicates:

"Thus the Jewish leaders had built up 'Zion with blood, and Jerusalem with iniquity' (Micah 3:10). . . . For nearly forty years after the doom of Jerusalem had been pronounced by Christ Himself, the Lord delayed His judgments upon the city and the nation. Wonderful was the long-suffering of God toward the rejectors of His gospel and the murderers of His Son. The parable of the unfruitful tree represented God's dealings with the *Jewish nation*. The command had gone forth, 'Cut it down; why cumbereth it the ground?' (Luke 13:7) but divine mercy had spared it yet a little longer." [26]

## WERE THE JEWS CURSED FOREVER?

The question sounds ludicrous 2,000 years after the event of the Crucifixion. And yet we should address it, since some Christians and among them some Seventh-day Adventists would support the idea. Ellen White is clear on the matter. Just as she acknowledges God's judgment on the "Jewish nation"(see quotation above from *The Great Controversy,* p. 27) she further explains why God waited ("divine mercy . . . spared it"). She gives the following reason:

"There were still many among the Jews who were ignorant

of the character and the work of Christ. And the children had not enjoyed the opportunities or received the light which their parents had spurned. Through the preaching of the apostles and their associates, God would cause light to shine upon them; they would be permitted to see how prophecy had been fulfilled, not only in the birth and life of Christ, but in His death and resurrection. *The children were not condemned for the sins of the parents; but when, with a knowledge of all the light given to their parents,* the children rejected the additional light granted to themselves, they became partakers of the parents' sins, and filled up the measure of their iniquity."[27]

We must here notice that "the children were not condemned for the sins of the parents." God's reluctance to implement His judgment underlies an important ethical principle: the curse is not effective upon them as long as they do not receive a "knowledge of *all* the light." In other words, the children of those who crucified Christ—and by extension all the Jews—are not rejected, they are not under the curse, as long as the Christian message in its *whole* light remains unavailable to them.

The question then arises: Had anyone presented the Christian message to the Jews in "all the light"? What about the Christian apostasy with regard to the law? Here Ellen G. White is unequivocal. She even makes a significant parallelism between the rejection of Christ by the Jewish rulers and that of the law by Christians.

"When the Jews rejected Christ they rejected the foundation of their faith. And, on the other hand, the Christian world of today who claim faith in Christ, but reject the law of God, are making a mistake similar to that of the deceived Jews."[28]

It is also significant that she uses the same technical term *(the great sin)* to designate both the rejection of Christ by Jews (the leaders) and the rejection of the law by Christians. The great sin of the Jews was their rejection of Christ; the great sin of the Christian world would be their rejection of the law of God, the foundation of His government in heaven and earth. For Ellen White, who associates Christ with the law, spurning the law amounts to a renunciation of Christ.

"The Christian church, on the other hand, who profess the utmost faith in Christ, in despising the Jewish system virtually deny Christ, who was the originator of the entire Jewish economy."[29]

The Christian church as a whole has dismissed the law, hence Christ. Thus, since the church has not presented the Jews with the truth in its "full light," it follows that as a whole the Jews have not yet been rejected.

## HOW WAS THE CURSE FULFILLED?

The crime of the Jewish leaders did not remain unpunished, however. Ellen White sees a twofold fulfillment of the curse they pronounced on themselves. It has already been realized at the fall of Jerusalem, hence the crumbling of the nation and as a consequence the scattering of the Jews. This fulfillment concerns the "Jewish nation" as a theocratic entity, one that has lost then its political unity.

"Terribly was it realized in the destruction of Jerusalem. Terribly has it been manifested in the condition of the Jewish nation for eighteen hundred years. . . . From land to land throughout the world, from century to century."[30]

More important, it will be implemented in heaven on the judgment day and will specifically concern the Jewish leaders.

"Terribly will that prayer be fulfilled in the great judgment

131

day. When Christ shall come to the earth again, not as a pris-
oner surrounded by a rabble will men see Him. They will see
Him then as heaven's King. Christ will come in His own glory,
in the glory of His Father, and the glory of the holy angels. . . .
Those who mocked and smote Him will be there. The *priests
and rulers* will behold again the scene in the judgment hall. Every
circumstance will appear before them, as if written in letters of
fire. Then those who prayed, 'His blood be on us, and on our
children,' will receive the answer to their prayer." [31]

## WHY DID THE JEWS SUFFER?

If the Jews are not under a curse, how can we explain the
tragedies they have endured throughout the centuries? For
Ellen White, this suffering has nothing to do with God.

"The heathen and those called Christians alike have been their
foes. Those professed Christians, in their zeal for Christ, whom the
Jews crucified, thought that the more suffering they could bring
upon them, the better would God be pleased. . . . They might be
looked upon as specially visited by the curse of God." [32]

The problem lies in fact on the level of human interpretation of the alleged divine curse. Human beings gave to the curse
the size it took—as a manifestation of their own hatred—to
confer upon their own deeds the seal of "divine" justification.

## PROPHECY AND ISRAEL

For Ellen White, not only had God not rejected the Jews,
but they were still to play an active role in the history of
humanity's salvation. She gave a prophecy that concerns the
future of Israel and the Jews, one characterized by a number
of specific features.

## 1. It Is a Prophecy About Jewish Israel.

It is first noteworthy that Ellen White's prophecy about the Jews is situated within a prophecy about historical Israel.

"To the ten tribes,[33] long rebellious and impenitent, was given no promise of complete restoration to their former power in Palestine. Until the end of time, they were to be 'wanderers among the nations.' But through Hosea was given a prophecy that set before them the privilege of having a part in the final restoration that is to be made to the people of God at the close of earth's history, when Christ shall appear as King of kings and Lord of lords."[34]

Note that in Ellen White Hosea's text is a real prophecy about Jewish Israel after the time of Christ. "Through Hosea was given a prophecy . . ." She is not simply quoting a verse as a proof text in homiletical fashion. Instead, she informs us under inspiration that the words of Hosea's prophecy *will be fulfilled in history,* and that it applies to the Jewish people in general, "the ten tribes, long rebellious and impenitent."

Elsewhere she underlines the prophecy's predictive nature. "There will be many converted from among the Jews, and these converts will aid in preparing the way of the Lord. . . . The predictions of prophecy will be fulfilled."[35]

## 2. Many Jews Will Be Converted.

Again, this prophecy does not agree with the dispensationalist view. It is not the whole people of David as a nation who will respond to God's covenant. Yet the numbers of converts will be significant enough to qualify as a "multitude," or "many."

"For there are to be a *multitude* convinced of the truth, who will take their position for God. The time is coming when there will be as many converted in a day as there were on the day of

Pentecost, after the disciples had received the Holy Spirit."[36]

"There will be *many* converted from among the Jews. . . . A nation shall be born in a day."[37]

"There are among the Jews many who will be converted, and through whom we shall see the salvation of God go forth as a lamp that burneth."[38]

*"Many* of the Jewish people will by faith receive Christ as their redeemer."[39]

### 3. This Conversion Movement Will Take Place at the End of Time.

For Ellen White, however, the period of such conversions had not yet arrived in her time. When someone asked her about the need for a mission to the Jews in the Old Jerusalem, she warned that it would distract "from the present work of the Lord."[40] Although she considered that some evangelism among Jews was already feasible and encouraged it, she definitely placed the conversion of the Jews and the success of Christian testimony among them chiefly in the future, at the time of the end:

"In the closing proclamation of the gospel, when special work is to be done for classes of people hitherto neglected, God expects His messengers to take particular interest in the Jewish people whom they find in all parts of the earth."[41]

"The work of which the prophet Zechariah writes is a type of the spiritual restoration to be wrought for Israel before the end of time."[42]

"Until the end of time, they were to be 'wanderers among the nations.' But through Hosea was given a prophecy that set before them the privilege of having a part in the final restoration that is to be made to the people of God at the close of earth's history."[43]

## 4. Israel Is Still God's People.

It is interesting to note in the context of her statements about large-scale conversions that she does not depict Jewish Israel as a rejected people, definitively banned from God. Instead, Ellen White describes the Jews in a situation of expectation. Again, referring to Hosea's prophecy, she concludes:

"'Many days,' the prophet declared, the ten tribes were to abide 'without a king, and without a prince, and without a sacrifice, and without an image, and without an ephod, and without teraphim.' 'Afterward,' the prophet continued, 'shall the children of Israel return, and seek the Lord their God, and David their king; and shall fear the Lord and His goodness in the latter days.'"[44]

Thus Jewish Israel belongs to a transitory stage, "for many days . . . without a king . . . without teraphim." That is, without a theocratic rule and yet still playing a role as a witness. Ellen White's characterization of the Jewish people during that time is significant. "In the last days of this earth's history, God's covenant with *His commandment-keeping people* is to be renewed."[45]

## 5. Converted Jews Will Have a Part in the Final Restoration.

This prophecy about Israel is not just about the Jews. It also has important implications for the world at large, because these converted Jews will play a significant role in the final proclamation of the three angels' messages.

"These converts will aid in preparing the way of the Lord, and making straight in the desert a highway for our God. Converted Jews are to have an important part to act in the great preparations to be made in the future to receive Christ, our Prince. A nation shall be born in a day. How? By men whom

God has appointed being converted to the truth."[46]

"There are Jews everywhere. . . . There are among them many who will come to the light, and who will proclaim the immutability of the law of God with wonderful power."[47]

## MISSION TO THE JEWS

From this prophecy about Israel, Ellen White consistently infers three subsequent lessons:

1. She sadly observes that Adventists have neglected the Jews.

2. She urges God's people to engage in the mission to the Jews.

3. She gives specific advice to prepare for the mission.

### 1. A Neglected Work

Ellen White does not just deplore the general indifference toward reaching Jews; she also denounces its deficiencies. "A little is being done, but it is nothing compared with what might be done. There is a decided failure to take hold of this work as we ought."[48] Furthermore, she sadly observes that "among Christian ministers there are only a few who feel called upon to labor for the Jewish people."[49] Such a lack of interest puzzles and troubles her. "It has been a strange thing to me that there were so few who felt a burden to labor for the Jewish people."[50]

### 2. A Call for Jewish Evangelism

First of all, Ellen White encourages God's people to become aware of their responsibility toward the Jews. "In the closing proclamation of the gospel . . . God expects His messengers to take particular interest in the Jewish people whom they find in all parts of the earth."[51] "There are Jews everywhere, and to them the light of present truth is to be brought."[52]

## 3. Counsels for the Mission to the Jews

Ellen White does not contend herself with reproaching, warning, and theories. She gets practical and presents us with a set of specific recommendations and advice to make such a mission work.

### A FULL TESTIMONY

For Ellen White, the conversion of the Jews is subject to the condition of an unaltered presentation of the gospel. "When this gospel shall be presented in its fullness to the Jews, many will accept Christ as the Messiah."[53] This summons for a serious and complete presentation of the truth is not just a call for responsibility. It implies that so far the Jews have not been given this opportunity, and it confirms the failure of the Christian testimony, underlining again the anticipatory position of Jewish Israel.

### A SPECIAL WORK

"The work for the Jews, as outlined in the eleventh chapter of Romans, is a work that is to be treated with *special* wisdom."[54] Considering the particular condition of the Jews today, after 2,000 years of anti-Semitism, Ellen White concludes dramatically that "our ministers need more of the wisdom that Paul had."[55] She then appeals for a "special effort." "Let there be special efforts for the enlightenment of the Jews."[56] That Ellen White uses the word "special" to systematically qualify the mission to the Jews suggests the need for a particular, different, and "better" attention toward this ministry.

### A STRATEGY OF RECONCILIATION AND LOVE—
### NOT OF REJECTION AND CONTEMPT

"We are plainly taught that we should not despise the Jews;

for among them the Lord has mighty men, who will proclaim the truth with power."[57]

"The work that Christ came to do in our world was not to create separating barriers and constantly thrust upon the people the fact that they were wrong. . . . Nor does Paul proclaim to the Jews a Messiah whose work it is to destroy the old dispensation, but a Messiah who came to develop the Jewish economy with the truth."[58]

"Paul did not approach the Jews in such a way as to arouse their prejudices."[59]

"Nor does Paul proclaim to the Jews a Messiah whose work is to destroy the old dispensation, but a Messiah who came to develop the whole Jewish economy in accordance with the truth."[60]

"As the Old Testament Scriptures are blended with the New in an explanation of Jehovah's eternal purpose, this will be to many of the Jews as the dawn of a new creation, the resurrection of the soul. As they see the Christ of the gospel dispensation portrayed in the pages of the Old Testament Scriptures, and perceive how clearly the New Testament explains the Old, their slumbering faculties will be aroused, and they will recognize Christ as the Savior of the world."[61]

## AN EXPLANATION OF MESSIANIC PROPHECIES

"In preaching to the Thessalonians, Paul appealed to the Old Testament prophecies concerning the Messiah. Christ in His ministry had opened the minds of His disciples to these prophecies; 'beginning at Moses and all the prophets, He expounded unto them in all the Scriptures the things concerning himself' (Luke 24:27). Peter in preaching Christ had produced his evidence from the Old Testament."[62]

## A PROGRESSIVE APPROACH

"Great wisdom should be used in the presentation of a truth that comes directly in opposition to the opinions and practices of the people. Paul's habit was to dwell upon the prophecies when with the Jewish people, and bring them down *step by step,* and then after some time open the subject of Christ as the true Messiah."[63]

## SHOULD INVOLVE "CONVERTED" JEWS

*"Converted Jews* are to have an important part to act in the great preparations to be made in the future to receive Christ, our Prince. A nation shall be born in a day."[64]

*"The Jews* are to be a power to labor for the Jews; and we are to see the salvation of God. We are altogether too narrow. We need to be broader-minded."[65]

## THE USE OF LITERATURE

In answer to a question from her son asking about the means we should use for the conversion of the Jews, she once answered: "I saw the literature scattered everywhere among the Jews, and when the pinch comes, God will move upon His messengers to gather in an abundant harvest."[66]

## THE CASE OF MARCUS LICHTENSTEIN

It is appropriate at this stage to mention Marcus Lichtenstein, a Jew who left the church because of the behavior of some people holding the highest positions in denominational organization. The incident was blatantly one of the most painful stumbling blocks in the mission to the Jews. Ellen White's reflection and rebuke on the incident are noteworthy.

"In a most remarkable manner the Lord wrought upon the

heart of Marcus Lichtenstein and directed the course of this young man to Battle Creek, that he might there be brought under the influence of the truth and be converted; that he might obtain an experience and be united to the office of publication. His education in the Jewish religion would have qualified him to prepare publications. His knowledge of Hebrew would have been a help to the office in the preparation of publications through which access could be gained to a class that otherwise could not be reached. It was no inferior gift that God gave to the office in Marcus. His deportment and conscientiousness were in accordance with the principles of the wonderful truths he was beginning to see and appreciate.

"But the influence of some in the office grieved and discouraged Marcus. Those young men who did not esteem him as he deserved, and whose Christian life was a contradiction to their profession, were the means that Satan used to separate from the office the gift which God had given to it. He went away perplexed, grieved, discouraged. Those who had years of experience, and who should have had the love of Christ in their hearts, were so far separated from God by selfishness, pride, and their own folly that they could not discern the special work of God in connecting Marcus with the office.

"If those who are connected with the office had been awake and not spiritually paralyzed, Brother Lichtenstein would long ago have been connected with the office and might now be prepared to do a good work which much needs to be done. He should have been engaged in teaching young men and women, that they might now be qualified to become workers in missionary fields."[67]

## CONCLUSION

Ellen G. White's comments on the Jews and Israel must be

handled with care, as she was approaching this issue from a spiritual perspective, either homiletically to take lessons from past history or prophetically within the framework of the time of the end. She addressed issues regarding real Jews only incidentally, as she encountered converted Jews such as F. C. Gilbert or M. Lichtenstein. It is also important to realize how much Ellen White's language reflected her historical situation. For instance, when she used the expression "Old Jerusalem" in her statement that "Old Jerusalem never would be built up"[68] she had in mind the biblical Davidic Jerusalem with all its messianic and theocratic claims, "the glorious city of the Lord during His millennial reign"[69] and not the "Old Jerusalem" of the modern state of Israel. Likewise, when she wrote about what she called "modern Israel,"[70] she could not have referred to the nation established years later, but she had in mind a "spiritual" understanding of Israel.

The way she confronted Christian injustices against the Jews and her frequent admonitions that "we should not despise the Jews,"[71] in addition to her readiness to correct herself and change her words to adjust to new meanings, suggests that today, after the Holocaust and the creation of the state of Israel, she would have expressed herself differently on these matters. Such observation makes it imperative that we interpret her writings in context, and should prevent us from a too literal and mechanical interpretation of her words.

---

[1] *The Desire of Ages,* pp. 618, 619. (Italics supplied.)

[2] *Christ's Object Lessons,* p. 306. (Italics supplied.)

[3] *Ibid.,* p. 293.

[4] *Ibid.,* pp. 293, 294. (Italics supplied.)

[5] *Ibid.,* p. 292.

[6] *Ibid.,* pp. 294, 295.

[7] *Ibid.,* p. 294.

[8] *Ibid.*

[9] *The Story of Redemption* (Washington, D.C.: Review and Herald Pub. Assn., 1947), p. 246.

[10] *Review and Herald,* Feb. 18, 1890. (Italics supplied.)

[11] *The Acts of the Apostles,* p. 375.

[12] *Ibid.,* p. 377.

[13] *The Great Controversy,* p. 27.

[14] *Ibid.,* p. 28.

[15] *Review and Herald,* Dec. 13, 1898. (Italics supplied.)

[16] *Review and Herald,* Feb. 20, 1900. (Italics supplied.)

[17] *Ibid.* (Italics supplied.)

[18] *Review and Herald,* Jan. 24, 1899. (Italics supplied.)

[19] *Review and Herald,* June 7, 1906. (Italics supplied.)

[20] *The Great Controversy,* p. 328. (Italics supplied.)

[21] *Spiritual Gifts* (Battle Creek, Mich.: James White, 1858), vol. 1, pp. 106, 107. (Italics supplied.)

[22] *Early Writings,* pp. 212, 213. (Italics supplied.)

[23] *Review and Herald,* Aug. 29, 1899.

[24] *Early Writings,* pp. 212, 213. (Italics supplied.)

[25] *Christ's Object Lessons,* pp. 294, 295.

[26] *The Great Controversy,* p. 27. (Italics supplied.)

[27] *Ibid.,* pp. 27, 28. (Italics supplied.)

[28] *Selected Messages,* book 1, p. 229.

[29] *Ibid.,* p. 232.

[30] *The Desire of Ages,* p. 739.

[31] *Ibid.* (Italics supplied.)

[32] *Early Writings,* pp. 212, 213.

[33] The concept of the 10 tribes should not be taken literally. When the kingdom of the north disappeared, many people from there joined the southern kingdom. Already the Bible tells us that many Israelites, revolted by the religious unfaithfulness of the north, fled to the Judean kingdom (2 Chron. 15). Thus the 10 tribes survived in the new entity represented by the southern kingdom. And beyond this physical survival, the 10 tribes were also maintained alive in a spiritual way. Scripture metaphorically uses the theme of the restoration of the 10 tribes to express hope when the prophets dreamed of the resurrection of the nation (Jer. 31:3, 5, 19; Eze. 37:15-28).

[34] *Prophets and Kings,* p. 298.

[35] *Evangelism,* p. 579.

[36] *Review and Herald,* June 29, 1905. (Italics supplied.)

[37] *Evangelism,* p. 579. (Italics supplied.)

[38] *Ibid.* (Italics supplied.)

[39] *Ibid.* (Italics supplied.)

[40] *Early Writings,* p. 75.

[41] *The Acts of the Apostles,* p. 381.

[42] *Manuscript Releases* (Washington, D.C.: Ellen G. White Estate, 1981–1993), vol. 1, p. 315.

[43] *Prophets and Kings,* p. 298.

[44] *Ibid.*

[45] *Ibid.,* p. 299. (Italics supplied.)

[46] *Evangelism,* p. 579.

[47] *Ibid.,* p. 578.

[48] *Manuscript Releases,* vol. 1, p. 137.

[49] *The Acts of the Apostles,* pp. 380, 381.

[50] *Evangelism,* p. 578.

[51] *The Acts of the Apostles,* p. 381.

[52] *Evangelism,* p. 578.

[53] *The Acts of the Apostles,* p. 380.

[54] *The Seventh-day Adventist Bible Commentary,* Ellen G. White Comments, vol. 6, p. 1079. (Italics supplied.)

[55] *Evangelism,* p. 141.

[56] *Manuscript Releases,* vol. 1, p. 138.

[57] *Ibid.,* p. 137.

[58] *Manuscript Releases,* vol. 1, pp. 137, 138.

[59] *Gospel Workers* (Washington, D.C.: Review and Herald Pub. Assn., 1915), p. 118.

[60] *Evangelism,* p. 554.

[61] *The Acts of the Apostles,* p. 381.

[62] *Ibid.,* p. 221.

[63] *Evangelism,* p. 246. (Italics supplied.)

[64] *Ibid.,* p. 579. (Italics supplied.)

[65] *Review and Herald,* June 29, 1905. (Italics supplied.)

[66] Reported by S. A. Kaplan in "Report of the Jewish Work."

[67] *Testimonies,* vol. 3, pp. 205, 206.

[68] *Early Writings,* p. 75.

[69] Joseph Marsh, in *Advent Harbinger,* Aug. 30, 1851, p. 85.

[70] *Testimonies,* vol. 2, p. 109.

[71] *Manuscript Releases,* vol. 1, p. 137.